Daniel C. Eddy

Our Travelling Party from the Baltic to Vesuvius

Vol. 1

Daniel C. Eddy

Our Travelling Party from the Baltic to Vesuvius
Vol. 1

ISBN/EAN: 9783337292270

Printed in Europe, USA, Canada, Australia, Japan

Cover: Foto ©Andreas Hilbeck / pixelio.de

More available books at **www.hansebooks.com**

OUR TRAVELLING PARTY

FROM

THE BALTIC TO VESUVIUS.

BY
DANIEL C. EDDY.

ILLUSTRATED.

BOSTON:
D. LOTHROP & COMPANY,
FRANKLIN ST., CORNER HAWLEY.

NOTE.

The next number of this series of books — "Over the Alps and down the Rhine" — will be issued in a few weeks, completing the tour of the Percy Family in Europe.

CONTENTS.

CHAP.		PAGE
I.	A Ride for Daylight.	11
II.	A Batch of Letters.	23
III.	Free City of the North.	34
IV.	How they do in Prussia.	47
V.	The Emperor's City.	66
VI.	The Wonderful Cave.	76
VII.	The Bride of the Sea.	86
VIII.	City of Artists and Flower Girls.	100
IX.	First Views of Rome.	116
X.	Pilgrimage to St. Peter's.	127
XI.	Walks around the Forum.	142
XII.	The Vatican, Inside and Out.	159
XIII.	The Carnival.	170
XIV.	Naples.	182
XV.	Climbing Vesuvius.	196
XVI.	The Buried Cities.	205
XVII.	Coastwise.	219
XVIII.	Glimpses of Battle.	232

ENGRAVINGS.

	PAGE
ST. PETER'S, ROME.	1
THE CA' DORA PALACE.	10
VENICE.	93
THE CAMPANILE, FLORENCE.	114
THE HOLY STAIRS.	138
THE ROMAN FORUM.	145
A STREET IN POMPEII.	214
THE DORIA PALACE.	227

THE CA' DORA PALACE, VENICE.

THE BALTIC TO VESUVIUS.

Chapter I.

A RIDE FOR DAYLIGHT.

AN American who can travel in his own country from the banks of the Kennebec to the shores of the Gulf of Mexico, from Plymouth Rock to San Francisco, without any change in the currency, or any examination of passports, or any custom house detention, is amazed in the old world by the frequency of the calls made for his passport, and at the number of dirty hands that are thrust into his carpet bag, and with the constant refusals of traders, porters, and hackmen to take the coin, which was current but a few miles distant. Those who visit Europe for the first time, and who have little or no experience in these matters, often express their disgust in a vehement manner, but after a time become so familiarized to the trouble and detention, that they bear it with philosophical coolness.

"What now?" asked Mr. Tenant, as the cars came to a sudden stop, nearly shaking him from his seat.

"I don't know," answered Walter. "We must wait and see."

"Wait, must we?" cried Minnie. "See, the people are getting out of the cars; and they are tumbling out the baggage."

"I think we had better be tumbling out," replied Walter.

When they had alighted from the carriage, they found they were at the custom house on the Prussian frontier, where an examination of the baggage took place, detaining them an hour, which caused no little complaint among the passengers, who were all in a hurry to get to their places of destination. But at length they were in the cars again, and on their way.

"Whew! how we go!" cried Walter, as they whirled through fields of grain, by towns and villages, across rivers, and through forests.

The afternoon and evening were spent in conversation about the places on the route, and the manners and customs of the people. Mr. Tenant, seeing the weariness of the whole party, did all he could to amuse them, and related many curious incidents of foreign travel. The children plied him with questions, all of which he was able to answer, as his reading had been varied and extensive. But as night came on, the young people fell asleep, and for a few hours not a word was spoken. About midnight, however, the train began to enter some city; and Walter, always on the alert to see what was going on, began to rub his eyes, and peer out into the darkness, where all was indistinguishable gloom.

"Where are we?" he asked.

No one answered.

"Min, I say, we are coming *somewhere*."

"We have been somewhere all day," answered Minnie.

"Yes, but we are coming to a great city. I should like to know what it is. I wish pa would wake up and tell us."

"Pa and Mr. Tenant are both in Dreamland."

"No, they are not."

"Where are they?"

"In the land of Nod."

The two gentlemen, who had overheard the conversation, laughed, and Mr. Percy remarked, "We are riding into Hanover."

"Shall we stop?"

"Two hours."

"What can we do?"

"We will decide when we get in."

And soon they were in the station house at Hanover, where they found a long refreshment room well lighted, and there they took supper. After supper, Mr. Percy said, "Now, shall we throw ourselves on these lounges and get a little sleep, or shall we go out and get a night view of the city?"

"Is there no danger here in the night?" asked the little girl.

"Danger! You are a brave girl!" said Walter.

"I am as brave as you are; but I don't want pa to go out here and get robbed, in the night."

"You speak one word for father, and two for yourself."

"I didn't think of myself."

"You are afraid."

"Pho!"

"I think there can be no danger," said Mr. Percy. "If Minnie is afraid, we will leave her with Colonel Sanborn and lady, who are taking supper in the other room."

"Ah, ha, afraid! That is funny."

"Well, then we will go out."

As they left the depot, Walter asked, "What is the city of Hanover noted for?"

"Not much," replied his father. "It is the

capital of the kingdom of Hanover, and is built in the form of a half moon."

They wandered about for some time, and at length sat down on a bench under some trees, near the palace which loomed up before them, and in front of which sentinels were slowly pacing backward and forward.

"I remember," said Walter to his father, as they sat there in the night air, "that you told us that one of the races of English sovereigns was styled the 'House of Hanover.'"

"Yes."

"Did that line of sovereigns originate here?"

"Yes."

"Well, how did they get to the throne of England?"

"By a very natural process."

"Please tell me about it."

"I will. The last of the house of Stuart was Anne."

"The one that was called 'the *good queen* Anne'?"

"The same."

"Why did they call her the *good* queen?" asked Minnie.

"Because she was a good wife and mother, and also a good queen, though she had many troubles during her reign."

"But what had she to do with the origin of the house of Hanover?" queried Walter.

"If you will not interrupt me again, I will tell you."

"I will not interrupt again."

"Well, on the death of Anne, George Lewis, the elector of Hanover, came to the throne. He was the son of Ernest Augustus and Sophia, granddaughter of James I."

"Ah!"

"He was the most direct heir to the throne, and ascended it in 1714, when Anne died."

"I understand."

"Understand what, Walt?" asked his sister.

"Why, what we were talking about, certainly, — the way in which the British throne was transferred from the house of Stuart to the house of Hanover."

"I think we had better return to the station," said Mr. Tenant, coming up to the group.

"Yes," replied Mr. Percy; "the children will get cold if they stay here much longer in the night air."

So they all moved towards the depot, which they found crowded with people, some lying down asleep, some smoking, some reading, and others gayly conversing together, or walking about. They met Colonel Sanborn and his wife, the latter of whom was as fussy as ever, declaring that she had had no sleep for a week, and was almost worn out with fatigue. Her husband seemed to take no notice of her complaints, but moved about very quietly attending to his baggage, and looking out for his wife's boxes and bundles.

At four o'clock in the morning, they all took cars for Hamburg. The Percy family all found seats in one carriage, and there being no other persons with them, they could converse freely; and as the children were wide awake, the two gentlemen had as much as they could do to answer questions.

Minnie made Mr. Tenant tell her all about the legend of the Flying Dutchman, interrupting him a dozen times to declare her scepticism as to the particulars, and ending with assuring the narrator that she did not believe a word of it. Walter was gathering facts from his father in relation to the places through which they passed, and with his map of Europe in his hand, he gained considerable information.

At length they arrived at the end of their railway ride, and the party at once began to gather up their bags and bundles, and leave the cars.

"O, I am so glad we are there?" cried Minnie.

"So am I," answered Walter.

"But we are not there, children," said Mr. Percy.

"Not there?"

"No."

"Then where are we?"

"Where do you think?"

"I don't know."

"Does this look like Hamburg?"

"No, not like what I expected Hamburg to be. What place is this?"

"It is Haarburg."

"Where is Hamburg?"

"Follow us, and you will see."

The children followed on to a carriage, into which they entered, and were driven to the bank of a river, where they found a steamboat just ready to start out, and they went on board of her. When they were all seated, Mr. Percy said,—

"This river is the Elbe, and Hamburg is a few miles distant. We shall reach the city in an hour."

The hour was very pleasantly spent on board the little steamer, which was crowded with all sorts of people. Minnie got a cool place in the shade, and Walter was on the lookout for any novel incident that might occur. Mrs. Sanborn screamed because a German trod on her long travelling dress, and gave him a scolding in English, of which he understood not a word; and he apologized in German, of which she knew not a syllable. Just as they reached the landing at Hamburg, Walter called out,—

"Father?"

"What say, my son?"

"Let me get a conveyance, and be guide to a hotel."

"I do not know as we can trust you."

"O, yes, you can. Don't tell me any thing, but let me try."

"Well."

Out he sprang, and soon returned with a man who was to carry out the baggage.

"Here, this way, Minnie; I have engaged a *droskie*," shouted Walter.

"A what?"

"A *droskie*."

"Mercy, the boy is crazy! Let me run and see what a *droskie* is."

The gentlemen laughed.

"Walter, where is the *droskie?*"

"This is it," replied Walter, pointing to a hackney coach which he had engaged.

The little girl sprang into the coach, and settled back into the soft cushions, laughing at what she termed Walter's attempt at showing off. The driver, having taken his seat, turned to get directions, looking inquiringly at the two gentlemen, who pointed to Walter.

"Drive to Hotel de l'Europe."

"*Yah!*"

Up one street and down another, through broad avenues and winding passages, they rode for a quarter of an hour, when the hack stopped before an elegant hotel on the Jungfernstieg, and the driver in great haste began to unstrap the baggage.

"Is this Hotel de l'Europe?" asked Walter, of the driver.

"*Yaw.*"

"Put on the baggage again! Put on the baggage, quick!" cried the lad.

"What now, Walter?" asked his father.

"The man is cheating us."

"How?"

"Why, this is Hotel Victoria."

"How do you know?"

"There is the name up there."

"Sure enough; but it is an elegant hotel. We had better stop here."

"O, no, sir; the man is trying to cheat us.

He is paid by the keeper. On with the baggage, driver."

The fellow, probably feed by the keeper of the hotel for every passenger brought to that house, put on the baggage in a surly manner, and drove to the right public house, which was but a short distance off, on a beautiful street called the *Alsterdam*. Mr. Tenant was about to leap out, when Walter stopped him.

"Wait, wait, sir; let me go in and engage apartments."

"Walter, you are a case," laughingly cried Mr. Tenant.

"A *show* case," suggested Minnie.

While he was gone in, Minnie said to her father, —

"I heard you call the street that the other hotel stands on, *Jungstrongferng*, or something of that kind."

"I called it *Jungfernstieg*," (pronounced *Yoongfernsteeg*.)

"Well, what does that mean?"

"It means 'Maiden's walk.'"

"Ah! then I will walk there."

Walter now appeared. He had engaged very fine apartments on the third floor, facing the Alster basin, and had secured them on very reasonable terms; and soon the party was severally engaged in bathing, unstrapping trunks, and shaving, and the usual employments of travellers for the first hour after arriving in the city; and thus we leave them occupied.

Chapter II.

A BATCH OF LETTERS.

"Rap, rap, rap," sounded on the door of Mr. Percy's room, about an hour after their arrival, as, with toilet duties performed, the whole party were gathered at one of the windows looking out upon the Alsterbasin, covered with little boats, and swans, whose long, white necks were stretched up or plunged deep beneath the surface.

"Rap, rap, rap."

"I guess somebody wants to get in, pa," said Minnie.

"Rap, rap, rap."

"Come in."

"Ze lettes for von gentlishman, vot sent porter!" exclaimed the servant, as he opened the door.

"Ah, yes, I sent to the post-office," said Mr. Tenant, taking a package of letters from the servant's hand.

"Hurrah!" was Walter's joyful cry.

"A lot of them," chimed in Mr. Percy.

"Cut the string, Mr. Tenant," cried Minnie.

That gentleman slowly untied the bundle, and looked over the letters.

"O, do be quick!" cried Minnie, impatiently.

"No hurry, child. Let me see — one for me; from Jenkins, probably."

"O, how provoking!"

"Another for me — from Har——"

"It's too bad!"

"One for friend Percy."

Mr. Percy took the letter.

"Two more for Mr. Percy."

"Who are the next for? I cannot wait."

"One two, three, for Walter."

"None for me."

"Yes, three for you, Min, and the rest are papers."

The children took the precious documents, and hurried away to their rooms to read them. The gentlemen opened theirs, and found them filled with business matters, and family affairs, and kind words from dear ones. But as they will not be likely to interest the reader, we will follow the children to Walter's room, where they are laughing and weeping by turns over the letters they had received.

"Here is one," said Walter, "written to you and me."

"Who is it from?"

"Mother!"

"O, do read that first."

Walter read his mother's letter, as follows:—

My Dear Children:—

Your constant letters are a source of much comfort while you are absent. We read them over and over again, and the children in the neighborhood come and take them away, and read them to each other. I think I can see a constant improvement in the style and construction of your letters. They are more natural and graceful, and win for you many compliments from those who see them. Our dear pastor, Rev. Mr. K——, remarked to a friend that week that Walter seems to be realizing more solid benefit from his journey than most *men* would. I tell you these things to stimulate you to do better still. Only that you are being benefited by the tour you are making, would enable me to endure the prolonged absence of my dear boy and girl.

I am also glad to hear from your father such good account of your conduct. He tells me that you do not put yourself forward, or intrude yourselves upon other people. This is well. A bold boy or a brazen girl will not be loved by those who come in contact with them. But a modest child will secure a ready way to every generous heart. I feared that hotel life, and a constant contact with travellers of all lands, would take away your humility, and the deference you have always paid to persons older and better informed than yourselves, and am pleased to hear that my fears were groundless.

* * * * *

Among the boys in this neighborhood there prevails a strong desire to visit Europe. Walter's letters are read by them, and not a few are coaxing their parents to take them to the old world. Harry St. Clair seems to be wild with excitement, and his mother told me yesterday that she must prohibit his reading any more of your descriptions of what you see. The boy don't know what to make of what you write.

* * * * *

Charlie, I think, has improved as much at home as you have abroad. He and Rover are constant friends, the dog attending him in all his excursions. Charlie says he can catch trout as well as Walter can, and his uncle Winthrop has promised to take him into the country, where he can fish all he knows how to. When you return you will find him much improved. He has grown tall, and at school is making rapid proficiency. Yet I think he is lonesome, and sighs for his brother and sister. Last night, when I put him to bed, he asked, —

"Mother, do you think Walter and Minnie pray away off there."

"Yes," I said, "I hope they do."

He thought a moment, and then asked, —

"What do they pray for?"

"They pray," I answered, "that God will keep them safe from harm, guard them from all dangers, make them good children, and return them, when the time arrives, to their home."

"But, mother, do you think they ever pray for *me*?"

I told him I thought you did pray for little Charlie; and then he made me talk about you until he went to sleep with smiles on his face. And now, dear children, remember the advice I have given you in my previous letters, and write as often as you can, even if it be but a very few lines.

Your Mother.

The passages left out of this letter relate to some family matters, and to certain directions as to the clothing of the young travellers. When Walter closed the letter, he sat some time looking out the window, while Minnie, with her head on her hand, was gently tapping the floor with her dainty little foot. She was first to break the silence.

"What a dear, kind, good mother we have, Walter!"

"Yes, she loves us very much."

"And we should love her, and be very kind to her."

"Certainly, for we do not know how long we shall have her."

"Have her?" asked Minnie, inquiringly, as her eyes filled with tears.

"She may not live long. I remember she herself said once, that——"

"O Walter, don't talk so; you make my heart ache."

"Well, we will read another letter. Here is one from Harry St. Clair:"—

CAMBRIDGE, 1858.

Heigh-ho, Walter! how are you? Your mother told me where I could direct a letter to you, and so I concluded to write. You may be having such a good time that you will not want to hear from home. I wish I could fly over to where you are. At first I did not believe what you wrote; but old Falkner (who, by the way, is savage as a tiger this summer) tells me that your descriptions are all facts, and ——

"Old Falkner!" interrupted Minnie; "that is a pretty way to talk about his school teacher."

"Very true, but Harry is a wild boy, and has not been trained very well."

"I should be ashamed to be so disrespectful to my teacher."

"So should I. Besides, Mr. Falkner is such a perfect gentleman, that I wonder Harry is not more respectful."

"Well, read on."

I have been asking my father to let me visit Europe, but the stingy old fellow says it will cost so much that he cannot afford it, and tells me that I must wait.

"Who does he mean by 'stingy old fellow,' Walter?" asked Minnie.

"His father, of course."

"His father?"

"Yes."

"Well, I would throw his letter out the window."

"No, let me read."

That is the way it always is — I must *wait*. But I am bound to have a good time at home. The other day, when the old man had gone to town, I went ——

"Who does he mean by 'old man'?"

"His father."

"What a heathen he is, speaking of his father thus!"

"Let me finish the letter."

"Go on."

I went into the stable, and harnessed the sorrel horse, and set off to ride. I got Frank Day, and Arthur Boyce, and Tom Fellows, and away we went down through the Port, over the bridge, into town, rattling over the pavements, until the old horse sweat and the old chaise rattled. Well, we were out three hours, when I thought it time to get home, lest I should get caught. As we were going over the bridge we saw a team right in the way before us, and wishing to do a brave thing, I went up close behind, and cried out, "Get out of the way, you old fashioned team, or I will run you down." The carriage drew up to one side of the road, and as we passed I put out my head, and who do you think was in the carriage? Why, my old man and your uncle Winthrop. The way I put my head back was a caution. He did not see me, and being engaged in conversation, did not notice Sorrel. I got back as soon as I could, and when he reached the house I was sitting under the old elm, whittling out a boat for your brother Charles.

Thus, you see, we are having high times — about as good as to be in Europe. We shall all be glad to see you home.

Harry St. Clair.

"Well, what do you think of that letter?"
"I am ashamed of it."
"Harry is a fast boy."
"He will be a ruined boy."
"I am afraid he will. But I have one more."

Walter : —

I am printing a letter to you, and Miss Wright, the teacher, says she will correct it. She don't mean "correct it" as she corrects the boys, but put in the stops, and dot the i's and cross the t's, and fix the capitals right. I don't see why you don't come home. We all want to see you, and Rose Thornton blushes every time your name is mentioned — so Harry St. Clair says. Most all the boys have been away this summer, and we have been nowhere but to hingham and hull — I ought to put a great H before hingham and hull.

I would like to have you see a boat Harry St. Clair has made for me. It is a buster, I tell you. It is two foot — feet long. The masts are not in, nor are the sails up; but when you come home it will all be done. If Minnie was here she could make the sails out of cotton cloth, and sew them on the spars — the things that go across, you know. Walter, how does Minnie look now? Mother said the other day that she had got to be a little woman, and I thought I would like to know how she looked — a little woman!

CHARLES.

"What does he mean about Rose Thornton, Walter?" asked his sister.

"Nothing."

"He does."

"Nonsense."

"You gallanted Rose Thornton home from the picnic last summer, and have sent her bouquets ever since."

"What of it?"

"Pretty for a boy like you!"

"You are a silly little girl; but read your letters to me."

Minnie then read her three letters, all of which were from her young schoolmates, and all breathed an affection for the little wanderer who once formed a part of the happy group.

These having been read and discussed, the brother and sister went into their father's room, where they found him with several American newspapers, which they looked over with as much interest as they had read their letters. Mr. Percy pointed them to several items of news that he thought would be of interest to them.

They were then called to a substantial dinner, after which they took a carriage and rode through the streets of Hamburg, looking at the public buildings, and at the houses of the people. They found a great difference in the streets, some of them being long, wide, and elegant, and others narrow, close, crooked, and filled with poor, mean habitations. The difference will be explained hereafter.

Chapter III.

FREE CITY OF THE NORTH.

EVERY person who visits Hamburg comes away with a pleasant impression of the city. Some parts of it resemble the towns in Holland, while other parts are fresh and new, more resembling the new part of Edinburgh. The morning after our party arrived they went out to see the objects of interest. As they entered the carriage Walter asked, —

" Why is Hamburg called a *free* city ? "

" What do you think ? "

" I do not know; but perhaps it is called a free city because no duties are levied on goods that are brought in."

" No, not that."

" I should have known better than that," said Minnie, " because our baggage was examined when we came in. If there were no duties, what would our baggage have been overhauled for ? "

" True enough; I did not think of that."

" There are," said Mr. Percy, " several *fre*

towns, known as such, because they have their own municipal regulations and officers, and are not subject to any power beyond themselves. Hamburg is one of them."

"What are the others?"

"Bremen, Lubeck, and Frankfort. There were others, but they have renounced their independence."

"How many inhabitants has Hamburg?"

"About one hundred and fifty thousand. What you thought was an examination of baggage when you came in was merely an express arrangement for marking it."

"But, father, some sections of this city look very new and some very old. This part through which we are driving is very ancient. About our hotel it is all new, and looks as if just built; how is that?"

"I can tell you. A great conflagration occurred here in 1842, which swept away a large part of the city. What is now the new part, is the old burnt district rebuilt."

"Ah!"

"Yes, the part burnt was as mean as that through which we are riding."

"How much was burnt?"

"The fire swept through sixty-one streets, and many courts, ways, and small avenues, and laid in ashes seventeen hundred and forty-nine houses."

" Tremendous! "

" In the burnt district were several large and elegant churches, which seemed but stubble in the sway of the flames."

" How long did it burn ? "

" It commenced on one Thursday, and was not checked until the following Sunday."

" How did they arrest it ? "

" At first they pulled houses down; then riddled them with cannon balls. At length, by advice of an English engineer, they used gunpowder, and blew them up."

" What a great calamity! "

" It seemed so at first, but it proved a great source of public improvement. All these new buildings have taken the place of old ones. The Alsterbasin has been much improved, and the city greatly benefited."

" Walter, Walter! " exclaimed Minnie.

" What say ? "

" See that girl ? "

" What girl ? "

" The one over there, with no bonnet on."

" What of her ? "

" Why, she has a little baby coffin under her arm."

"So she has."

"That is queer. Is she going to bury it?"

"I don't know. I will ask pa."

"Father," he continued, "there is a girl over there with a little coffin under her arm — what is she going to do with it?"

"That is not a coffin, my son."

"Not a coffin?"

"No, if you look about you will see many such girls."

"Yes, Walter," said Minnie, "there is another, and another. There are several of them."

"I see. What and who are they, father?"

"They are servant girls, and what seems to be a coffin under the arm is a long basket; and if you could take off the shawl, you would find the basket filled with articles for the table."

"But they are all alike. The shawls that cover the baskets are all alike."

"True; all of these girls you see are dressed alike — a lace cap, kid gloves, and pretty shawl. The better circumstanced the young woman is, the neater she will be attired, but in the same general style."

"That is a singular custom."

"Yes; and it is a custom that prevails all through Germany. When you see one of them, you know she is a housemaid or cook."

"Among us this class of persons would not like to wear any thing to indicate their station, but would conceal all evidence of it."

"Generally that would be the case, but here it is the reverse. The housemaids choose to be known as such, as it distinguishes them from classes in still more humble condition."

The carriage now stopped before a church, and as Walter looked up he said, "This is one of the tall steeples."

"I should think so," replied his father.

"What church is it?"

"St. Michael's."

"Is the steeple as high as St. Paul's in London?"

"Yes; about one hundred feet higher."

"How many feet is this?"

"Can you not tell, if this is one hundred feet higher than St. Paul's?"

"Let me see. St. Paul's is about three hundred and fifty feet, so this must be about four hundred and fifty feet."

They had now entered the church, and as they gazed about, Minnie asked, —

"What have you brought us here for? I don't see any thing of interest."

The church at this moment shook with the thunder of a cannon.

"That is why we have come here," replied Mr. Percy; "let us go at once into the steeple."

"I don't understand yet."

"Do you know, Walter?"

"I think I do, sir."

"Then explain to your sister."

"What is it, Walter?"

"Why, this steeple is the tallest in the city, and on that account is used as a watch tower. A man is on the lookout from this steeple day and night. When he sees a fire he discharges his cannon. That is what you heard."

"Is there a fire in the city now?"

"Yes; but here we are at the watch station."

Here they found a man holding a flag with some figures on it, which indicated the direction of the fire. They looked, and saw, about a half mile distant, the red flames curling up from a small wooden building. They also saw the people flocking in that direction, and the engines at work at the fire.

Leaving this church they went to St. Nicholas, a large, unfinished edifice, in the Hapfenmarkt, to the Börse, where they found London and New York papers, and the steps of which were covered with flower girls selling flowers and fruit; to the Rathhaus, where they saw the offices of the city officials, and to many other places.

Several days were spent in Hamburg, in looking about the streets, walking around the Alster-basin, sailing on the Alster, and in riding about the environs, which are very pleasant.

One morning Mr. Percy said to Walter, " My son, have you any places you wish to go to before we leave Hamburg?"

" Yes, sir; I was told that some eminent men were born here, and if so, I would like to see where they lived."

" What men of eminence do you refer to?"

" Mr. Falkner told me, before I left home, that the poet Klopstock lived here."

" He did live here thirty years, and his house still stands."

They took a droskie and rode to Königistrasse, where they found the house. They then went to the house in which Felix Mendelssohn Bartholdy was born. Minnie wanted to know who these two persons were; she had never heard of them. Her father gave her all the particulars in his possession, in which she was much interested.

Thus day after day was spent. The city was so attractive that they lingered there some time. Their stay, however, was quite abruptly terminated by a new proposal made by Mr. Tenant, who, one morning at breakfast, after a long silence, said,—

"I have a notion."

"Is it a Boston notion?" asked Minnie.

"No."

"Or a Yankee notion?"

"No."

"Well, tell us, do; you men are such teasers."

"My notion is, that we had better go farther north. That is not in our plan, but we had better do it."

"How far?" asked Mr. Percy.

"To Copenhagen."

"What country is that in?" asked Minnie of Walter.

"In Denmark."

The plan pleased all the company but Minnie, who did not like the idea of going northward; but it was voted to go. So, leaving the mass of the baggage at the hotel in Hamburg, they rode in the cars to Kiel, where they took a steamer for Copenhagen. The voyage over the Baltic Sea was delightful. None of the party were seasick, and they arrived safely in Denmark, where they had a most delightful time. Then, crossing over into Sweden, they spent a week in that country. They found some difficulty in making the people understand what they wanted, and various amusing adventures and curious mistakes added interest to the excursion. When they had seen enough of these countries, they set out for Hamburg, where they arrived late one cloudy evening.

The next morning was the Sabbath, and the day dawned clear and beautiful. The whole city seemed asleep, for the quiet of holy time had settled upon it.

"Where shall we go to-day?" asked Mr. Tenant, as they all assembled at the breakfast table.

"We must try to improve the day some how?" answered Mr. Percy.

"I'll tell you where I'm going," cried Minnie.

"Where, Min?" asked her brother.

"To bed."

"What, in the daytime?"

"Yes."

"What for?"

"I am all tired out, and must rest."

"Are you afraid to stay here alone?"

"Afraid of what, sir knight?"

"Of being carried away."

"Ha, ha! that is funny!"

"We can leave Minnie at home," said her father.

"But where shall we go?"

"To some church."

"I know, pa; that missionary who was in

America a few years ago is here; we can go to his church."

" Who ? " asked Mr. Tenant.

" What missionary ? " asked Mr. Percy.

" Mr. Oncken."

" O, yes, I have seen and heard him. I like the idea," said Mr. Tenant.

So they went out after breakfast to see if they could find the chapel of the missionary. This they did without much difficulty, as Mr. Oncken is widely known and highly esteemed. In a humble street, they saw, over the door of a plain building, the words, " Baptesten Kapelle," and on entering a yard soon found the place. The chapel is a long, narrow room, capable of seating about three hundred persons. It was very full, and during the whole service the people were very attentive. Almost every person had a Bible, and when the preacher referred to any particular passage, they turned to the place and read after him. Walter was amused by seeing that the men and women did not sit together, but the men sat on one side of the house and the women on the other.

At the close of the service, the gentlemen went forward and addressed the missionary, who gave them a very kind welcome, as soon as he knew they were from America. At his request they accompanied him to his home, just outside of the city, where they found him delightfully located; and wishing him much success in his work, they took leave of him. As they left him, he gave Walter a beautiful picture, to keep as a memento of his visit.

When they arrived at the hotel they found Minnie sitting by the window, looking at her watch, which lay before her, with the crystal broken, the hands off, the case indented, and the thing otherwise injured.

"Ah, what is the matter, Min?" was her brother's salutation.

"Matter enough, I think."

"What is the trouble?"

"Don't you see?"

"I see your watch broken to pieces."

"Well, that is the matter."

"How did you do it?"

"I'll tell you. You see I had been lying down, and when I awoke I took my watch, and was tossing it by the chain, when the clasp gave way, and the watch went bang against the wall."

"That was downright carelessness."

"I was not hardly awake."

"If you had been sound asleep you should have used your watch better than that."

"Well, there it is; father, can it be mended?"

"Yes."

"O, well, that will make it all right."

"It may restore the watch," said Mr. Percy, "but it will not atone for your carelessness."

"I couldn't help it."

"Yes, my daughter, you could. You were throwing the watch about, and using it in an improper manner."

"It will not cost much to mend it."

"That makes no difference. You should take care of your watch, and your clothing, as if you were obliged to earn the money for them yourself."

"Well, pa, overlook it this time, and I will try and be more careful in future."

The evening of this Sabbath day was spent by our travellers at their rooms, in talking about home, and the dear friends far away over the ocean.

On Monday forenoon Minnie's watch was repaired, the hotel bills were settled, a few necessary articles purchased, and several calls made. After dinner the children were urged by their father to get a few hours sleep, as they were to ride in the night. At first they were unwilling to do so, but Mr. Percy urging the matter, they consented, and slept three or four hours, and about dark awoke much refreshed. A little before midnight they started for Berlin, preferring to ride in the cool night, rather than in the heat of day. It was dark, and the windows of the cars were small, and they saw nothing on the way. The train went whirling on through darkness until day-dawn, when the wheels ceased to turn, and our travellers found themselves in the capital of Prussia. Here new and strange scenes awaited them. Customs and habits which they had not met with before surprised and delighted them, and they were in just the state of mind to be pleased with every change. It would be hard to tell which enjoyed this journey most, the gentlemen or their youthful companions. Walter was sure that he was reaping the most pleasure and profit from the trip, while Minnie declared that no person ever derived as much good from a tour in Europe as she did; while the fresh color in the face of Mr. Percy gave evidence that he was much benefited.

Chapter IV.

HOW THEY DO IN PRUSSIA.

WE are to crowd a kingdom into a single chapter, and that a kingdom that occupies a central position, and has a commanding influence among the nations of Europe.

Our travellers were at a comfortable hotel in the city of Frederick the Great, the people of which were just pouring out from their homes to the business of the day.

"What have you ordered, Walter?" asked his father, as the lad came in from the office.

"A bath, a breakfast, and a droskie, sir."

"All at once?"

"No, sir; the bath now; the breakfast in an hour; the droskie at nine o'clock."

"Very well."

The bath was taken, and soon breakfast was eaten, and the droskie came to the door. It was decided that a few hours should be spent in riding about the city, seeing the outside of things, and becoming acquainted with the general appearance of the place. As they rode around, a *valet de place* pointed out the objects of interest, and gave such information as the party needed, they meanwhile being engaged in conversation.

"What street is this?" asked Minnie, as they rode through a beautiful avenue.

"This," replied her father, "is the celebrated *Unter der Linden*."

"Why so called?"

"Can you not tell?"

"No."

"Can you, Walter?"

"Yes, sir, I have heard. Besides, if I had not, I should have known. The street derives its name from these beautiful rows of Linden trees."

"That is right; the name signifies *under the Linden trees;* and the street is said by the people here to be the most beautiful on the continent."

"Who is king, father?" asked the boy.

"Frederick William IV."

"Is he an able monarch?"

"No, quite otherwise."

"Please tell us all about him."

"For a long time the king has been in an idiotic state, and the kingdom is governed by the prince regent."

"How came he idiotic?"

"When he came to the throne, being incapable of sustaining himself, he left the offices of state to others, and fell into habits of intemperance. His queen, a woman of much more character than her husband, for a long time concealed his faults, but with all her ingenuity the fact of his idiocy came out."

"There are," said Mr. Tenant, joining the conversation, "many good stories told of this king, growing out of his demented state."

"O, tell them," said Minnie; "tell them, if they are funny."

"One thing I have read is this: 'There exists still an old custom at Potsdam, according to which the fishermen once in the year pay to the king an old feudal tribute of fish. On that occasion, the queen, to prove to the mass of the people the falsehood of the rumors then freely circulating as to the state of the royal mind, dared to invite the foremost of these men to a fish dinner, to be presided over by the king himself. In fact, the dinner went off pretty well, the king muttering some words learned by rote, smiling, and, on the whole, behaving properly. The queen, anxious lest the scene so well got up should be spoiled, hastened to give the guests the signal of departure, when all at once the king rose, and in a thundering voice, demanded to be put in the frying pan.' This story I give you just as I read it."

" Do you believe it?"

" More than likely it is true."

" Tell us another."

" It is said that on the occasion when the Queen of Portugal celebrated her nuptials at Berlin by proxy, the king——"

" Plague take the French," cried Minnie; "what does *by proxy* mean."

"It is not French, I know," interposed Walter.

" What is it?"

" English."

" What does it **mean**?"

" By another."

" Well, go on; I won't interrupt again."

" 'The king was to have publicly assisted at the church ceremonies. Every thing was ready, and ministers, aides-de-camp, courtiers, foreign ambassadors, and the bride herself, were waiting for him, when, all at once, despite the desperate efforts of the queen, he was overtaken by the hallucination of believing himself the bridegroom. Some queer remarks he dropped as to his singular destiny in being married again during the lifetime of his first spouse, and as to the impropriety of his (the bridegroom's) appearance in a military uniform, left his exhibitors no chance but to countermand the spectacle which had been announced.'"

"That is a good one," exclaimed both children at once.

"I have another," said Mr. Tenant.

"What is it?"

"When it was seen that the king could not be retained in Berlin with safety, he was sent, under keepers, to Italy. He made some stay in the beautiful city of Florence, and there the following story is told of him: 'The royal patient was perfectly sane all day, received his guests, chatted, laughed, and was quite jolly; the dinner was announced, the company marched in; the king, of course, took his place at the head of the table, and every body waited for him to set the example to put their spoons in their mouths. But instead of doing what was expected of him, his majesty deliberately washed his face in the soup, and then sat complacently smiling on his friends, the long strings of vermicelli hanging down over his eyes and nose, and in his hair and mustache. You may imagine the effect; no one dared to laugh, however, and they had to sit out the dinner with this ridiculous figure-head, covered with gravy, (for he sternly refused towels,) talking to them all the while.'"

"What an old simpleton! ha, ha, ha!" was the response of Minnie.

"A funny king he must have been," was Walter's answer.

Just then a shouting was heard, a handsome carriage was seen dashing down the street, and the droskie driver drew up to one side.

"What now?" asked Mr. Percy.

"The prince! The prince!" replied the *valet de place.*

"The young prince?"

They were soon satisfied, for the Prince Frederick William, and his young wife, the princess royal of England, came driving by. The carriage in which they rode was an open one, and our travellers had a fine opportunity to see them. The princess was richly, but plainly dressed, and Minnie declared at once that she looked like her queen mother, only was much prettier.

The intense heat now admonished them to return to the hotel, where they rested the remainder of the day, writing letters to friends, or from the window of the hotel watching the passing crowds.

The several succeeding days were devoted to the objects of interest in Berlin. The Royal

Palace, an odd old structure, took up one day. The exterior of the building is very mean, but the interior is one blaze of wealth. The throne room, the several state apartments, are all decorated in the most costly style; one of them having been recently repaired, at an expense of six hundred thousand dollars. This whole palace abounds with curious things, and a visit to it is of the utmost interest. In the throne room is a large metallic music gallery, much resembling silver. In the time of Frederick the Great, the gallery was not imitation, but massive silver. But that monarch, at the close of one of his wars, wanting money, took this gallery down, and replaced it by its imitation substitute, melting the bars, posts, and ornaments, much to the wonder of the ignorant people, who could not conceive where the monarch obtained so much money in such hard times.

As they wandered about in this palace, Walter asked, —

"Have I not read that this building was haunted?"

"Haunted?" screamed Minnie, at the top of her voice, causing a party of English ladies and gentlemen, near by, to look and laugh.

"Yes, haunted, Min."

"If it is, let me get out."

"If it is haunted, Minnie, the ghost will not trouble you," said Mr. Tenant.

"Why not?"

"Because it only appears when a member of the royal family dies, and then only to some member of the royal family."

"Do you believe it?"

"Of course not. But the story is, that just before the death of any member of the royal family, the White Lady, as she is called, appears to any one of the family that may enter the building. Of course it is only a foolish superstition."

Another day was spent in the great national Museum. Minnie, who was ill that day, did not go; and when the party returned, Walter told her what they had seen.

"Come, Walter," she said, "sit down and tell me what you have seen, and where you have been."

"Well, we have been to the Museum, and have seen lots of things."

"What?"

"Why, first, the building was very beautiful, built about twenty years ago. Then we saw hosts of paintings and statues, that it would take me till to-morrow morning to describe."

"What else?"

"Close by this Museum is another, called the New Museum, connected with the old one by a bridge over a street."

"What was there?"

"A collection of Egyptian curiosities, deities, coins, household utensils, and ——"

"Any mummies?"

"Yes, plenty of them."

"What else?"

"A mineral museum, an anatomical collection, and a zoölogical collection."

"You must have had a time! What a pity that I have lost the day!"

"Something else we saw."

"What?"

"When we were walking about, a man, who could talk English but imperfectly, came to father and said, 'Come here, and for a franc I will show you something.' Father gave him the franc, and he led us to a little oratory at the end of a long room, and drawing aside a curtain, showed us a wax figure of Frederick the Great."

"How was he dressed?"

"He had on the same clothes he wore on the day he died; his old sword hangs by his side, and he looks just as he did when alive."

"How do you know? Did you see him when alive?" asked Minnie, with a quiet smile.

Walter bit his lips, and replied, —

"I can form an opinion as to how he looked"

"What else did you see?"

"Something you would like to have seen."

"What? Tell me!"

"The military hat of Napoleon, and several other articles found in his carriage when he retreated from Waterloo."

"How did they get to Berlin?"

"Blucher took them while pursuing the French."

"Well, what else?"

"Several things too numerous to mention, among which was a helmet, worn by an elector of Brandenburg, weighing twenty pounds; a watch, big as a turnip, and as worthless, once owned and carried by Frederick the Great; and many other things."

A call to dinner broke off the description of the day's work that was being given by Walter, and Minnie went to the table, declaring that she would not be ill again; for when she was sick, and did not go out, the party were sure to see something that she wanted to see.

It would take a long time to tell all our travellers saw while they were at Berlin. One day they visited the distinguished Baron Humboldt, to whom Mr. Percy had letters of introduction, and who received them with much courtesy. Another day was taken up by a visit to Potsdam. Potsdam is to Berlin what Hampton Court and Windsor Castle are to London, or Versailles and St. Cloud to Paris. Here are four palaces, and it is the summer residence of the royal family. The scenery all around is exquisite, and the drive-ways among the finest in the world. It is intimately connected with the memory of Frederick the Great, who expended large sums of money to make it one of the finest places on earth. Here are shown to the traveller the apartments of Frederick the Great, just as they were when he was alive, his inkstand all covered with ink, his chair and lounge, the mean little truck bed on which he slept, his books, and green eye-shade, just as when he laid them aside before going out to give up his account to God. The king was buried here, in the principal church. His plain metallic coffin lies above the ground. Once his sword was laid upon the coffin, but Napoleon carried it away; and to retaliate, the Prussians have hung the tomb with trophies taken by Blucher at Waterloo.

The morning before the party were to leave Berlin, Mr. Percy said, "We have now seen about all we can here; where can we ride to-day out of the city?"

"I think," answered Mr. Tenant, " that an excursion to Charlottenburg would be pleasant."

" How far is it, and which way ? "

" It is out through the Brandenburg gate, some few miles in the country."

" Let us go," said Walter.

" Yes, let's go," said Minnie.

So it was decided to go; a carriage was called, they all entered it, and soon arrived at the village, which lies on the Spree. Here are several palaces and monuments. They were particularly interested in the monument to the memory of Queen Louisa, a very beautiful but unfortunate woman.

Returning from the country, the party rode out to an eminence known as the Kreutzberg, where the best view of the city is obtained; and for a while they stood on the hill, at the foot of an iron cross, erected as a memorial of the recovery of independence from the French, gazing upon the city, as the beams of the sinking sun gilded its towers and domes with lines of beauty.

The following morning they started for Dresden. The country through which they rode was delightful. The grain was waving in the fields and the reapers went singing to their tasks.

"What are you thinking about, Mr. Tenant," asked Minnie, laying her hand on the shoulder of that gentleman, as he sat in silence looking out of the window of the car.

"I was thinking, coz, that this country was a paradise for lazy men."

"Then why don't you get a country seat and settle down? O, forgive me; my tongue went off without meaning any thing."

Mr. Tenant laughed, and pleasantly boxed the ears of the chatterbox, while her father looked grave.

"Why is this a paradise for lazy men?" she asked, coaxingly.

"Because I see, as we ride along, that the women do the work in the house and in the field, while the men seem to be lounging about on the fences, smoking and idling."

"I have noticed that ever since we have been upon the continent," replied Mr. Percy.

Six hours' ride brought them to Dresden, where they were to stop a few days. And pleasant days they were, spent among the picture galleries and museums. These are very numerous and very rich. The gentlemen thought they needed months to see all, while the children were content to walk quietly through. What pleased them most were the *Green Vaults*.

"The green vaults! what are they?" asked Minnie, as she heard her father speak of visiting them.

"O, you will see," was the reply.

"They must be vaults where wine is stored; I don't care about going."

As they approached the vaults, Mr. Percy explained.

"The green vaults are a suit of rooms in the palace."

"Under ground?" queried Minnie.

"No."

"What is in them?"

"They are filled with jewels, that for centuries have been collected by Prussian princes."

"Whew!"

They reached the vaults, and paying a fee at the door, entered. They found the first vault, or apartment, filled with bronze works; the second with curious ivory articles; the third with Florentine mosaics and carved works; and the others with precious stones, gold and silver trinkets, and rare and costly jewels. The children had seen the crown jewels of England, and several rich collections of gold and precious stones, but nothing like this.

"What is that?" asked Minnie of the inspector, as he held up a gold egg before the party.

"That," he said, " is a golden egg sent to a Saxon princess by her lover. For a long time she did not know its value, nor the purpose for which it had been sent. But one day, as she thought of her lover, she pressed it to her lips, and as she did so touched a secret spring, and the egg opened, and out dropped a golden yolk. Time rolled on, and by accident another secret spring was touched in the yolk, and that opened, and out dropped a golden chicken. Another spring was found, and the chicken opened, and out dropped a golden crown, set with diamonds. The crown also had a spring, and when that was touched, a marriage ring was found in it."

"A princely present truly," said Walter, as he almost held his breath with wonder.

"But we have many things more rare than that," said the inspector. "There, look at that."

"What is it?"

"The court of the Grand Mogul."

"What does it represent?"

"It represents the Emperor Aurengzebe on his throne, surrounded by his soldiers and courtiers."

"Who made it?"

"Dinglingler, a famous artist."

"How long did it take him?"

"Eight years."

"Wasted time," exclaimed Mr. Tenant.

"No, no!" replied the inspector, promptly.

"What did it cost?"

"Fifty-eight thousand dollars."

"O!" exclaimed Minnie, in surprise.

"After all, it only looks like a child's play house," said Walter.

They then saw huge heaps of silver and gold, golden chains and collars, sapphires, emeralds, rubies, pearls, and diamonds. As they were looking at the rings, the inspector said,—

"Here are two that belonged to the greatest man of Germany."

"Who was that?" asked one of the party.

"Martin Luther."

"Luther's rings!" exclaimed both of the children at once.

"Yes, children."

He handed out one for them to see. It was a cornelian, with a rose, and in the centre a cross. The other had on it a death's head and motto.

"This," said the inspector, "was his signet ring."

"What is the motto?" asked Walter.

His father read, "*Mori sæpe cogita.*"

"What does that mean?"

"Have you not a lexicon in the trunk?"

"Yes, a small one of French and Latin words."

"Well, see if you cannot study out the meaning of the motto. If you cannot, I will help you. The motto is important."

The party remained in the vaults, wondering at every step at the riches they saw piled up there, of no use to any one.

The next day they went on to Prague, arriving at that city about sunrise. When they left the Dresden depot, it was full of people sitting around little tables, eating, and drinking, and singing, and having a good time in a peculiar German way. The morning found them in the quiet Bohemian city, looking about for objects of interest.

"Can Walter tell us what there is here worth seeing?" asked Mr. Tenant, as they took a carriage to ride about.

"There are a convent, a cathedral, and a palace."

"Well, let us be about our work."

They went to the cathedral, and climbed at once to the top of the steeple, from which a grand view is obtained. The River Moldau winding through the town, spanned by several beautiful bridges; the sixty unique steeples of the place, all in view; the red roofs shining in the summer sun; and the hills beyond, crowned with fortifications, or sheltering neat convents,—form a noble panorama, and give one a fine idea of the Bohemian capital. They went into the cathedral as they came down. The most conspicuous object there is the shrine of John of Nepomuk.

"Who was he?" asked Minnie, as they stood before the shrine.

"He was the patron saint of Bohemia, and came to a violent death."

"How?" asked Walter.

"It is supposed that the queen was faithless to her husband, and with her conscience harrowed, discovered her sins to the confessor. The king, becoming suspicious, and not knowing how to test his doubts, applied to the monk, who refused to tell any thing that had been told him. The enraged husband had him drowned in the Moldau, and he is now revered as a saint and a martyr.

"What are these?" cried Minnie, who had gone on in advance of the group.

"They are relics of the old times of persecution," said the *valet-de-place*, pointing to a piller, chain, ring, and some other instruments of torture.

"How did they use them?" asked Walter.

"I will tell you. The ball you see was heated red

hot, and put into the hand of a person accused of heresy; if he held it calmly, and did not cry out, he was deemed innocent; if he groaned as the hissing iron burnt into the bones, it was a sign of his guilt."

"Horrible! horrible!" exclaimed the children.

They then went to the Church of San Loretto, where the monks have accumulated treasures to the amount of one million five hundred thousand dollars, and to various public buildings, all of which have an historic interest; and left one night for Vienna, with pleasant impressions of the fine old city of Prague.

Chapter V.

THE EMPEROR'S CITY.

"WON'T the Austrians ill-treat us, pa," asked Minnie, as they entered Vienna.

"Ill-treat us? What makes you think so?"

"I have always heard that they were a savage, cruel people, and was afraid we should meet with trouble."

"No, little puss, you need not fear that. You will be treated as well in Vienna as in Paris. I have been told that there is more genuine hospitality in Austria than in France."

"Well, then, what makes people always fear and hate the Austrians?"

"I don't know that they always do hate and fear them."

"At any rate, is there not an impression that they are barbarous?"

"Yes."

"What does it arise from?"

"Perhaps from the fact that the government here is very despotic."

"Who is king?"

"Austria is an empire, and has an emperor."

"Who is he? What is his name?"

"Francis Joseph."

"I have heard," said Walter, "the family that occupy the Austrian throne called the 'house of Hapsburg.' Where did that name come from?"

"There was a castle standing on the banks of the Aar, on a steep rock. It was called Habichtsburg."

"What does that mean?" asked Minnie.

"Hawks castle. The name gradually was changed to Hapsburg. The owners of the castle were called counts of Hapsburg. They were warlike, and constantly added to their territory. At length one of them, Rodolph, became Emperor of Germany. That was several hundred years ago."

"Then Rodolph founded the Hapsburg line of emperors?"

"Yes."

"I am glad I know; I have often asked, but no one could tell me."

Thus conversing, they reached the hotel of Archduke Charles, where they were to find a home for a few days. They found servants who could speak English, and plenty of men who wished to show them about the city. But as they had been riding all night, and were very weary, they preferred to rest all that day.

The next was the Sabbath, and after breakfast they went out, and wandered into the cathedral, an old edifice built in 1144, with a steeple four hundred and twenty-eight feet high. As they entered, a fine chime of bells were making music on the air.

"Hush, Walter! let us listen," said Minnie, stopping.

"To what?"

"To the beautiful bells."

"Did you ever hear about this chime?" asked Mr. Tenant.

"No," replied both children.

"I am told they were cast from one hundred and eighty cannon taken in wars."

"Who from?"

"The Turks."

"Push on, Walter," said his sister; "people are looking at us."

As they entered, they all paused, as the fine effect of the interior struck them. The large organ was sounding its melodious strains through the dim old arches. Thousands of people were sitting or kneeling in the body of the church. Several gayly robed priests were chanting at the altar. Pictures and statues of saints and angels looked down from the wall. The dim religious light came stealing through the windows, and the whole effect was gorgeous in the extreme. Of course they could not understand much of the service, and soon retired. Leaving the cathedral, they went to some other churches, and among them to the Church of the Capucines, where lies entombed young Napoleon, Duke of Reichstadt.

"What Napoleon, father?" asked Minnie, as they stood in the church.

"The son of the great emperor."

"But how came he here?"

"You know his mother was ——"

"Josephine?"

"No, dear, but Maria Louisa, eldest daughter of the Emperor Francis I. and Maria Theresa. When Napoleon abdicated the French throne, his queen retired to Austria, and renouncing the title of empress for herself, and the heirship to the throne for her son, entered upon the administration of the little duchy of Parma, while the young prince remained in Vienna until his death."

They also went to the Church of St. Augustine, where they saw a noble monument to the Duchess Christiana, by Canova, the death chapel of Leopold II., and the Loretto chapel, where the hearts of the emperor's family, and several others, are preserved in urns of gold.

In the evening of the Sabbath they walked out together, Mr. Percy with Walter, and Mr. Tenant with Minnie. Hardly knowing where they went, they got out upon the outskirts of the city, and found themselves in the midst of vast pleasure grounds, where all kinds of sports were being enjoyed by the Sabbath-breaking people. There were thousands of persons on the grounds, and fandangoes, mimic theatres, wooden horses, mock rifle shooting, dancing, singing, and drinking, were found in all directions. They looked on for a few minutes, and then hurried from the scene.

"Children," said Mr. Percy, "what effect did this sport have on you?"

"I thought it very silly," replied Minnie.

"I thought it very wicked," said Walter.

"Did either of you wish to stay and see it?"

"No," answered both in one voice.

"When you see such things going on, do you not sometimes wish they were prevalent in America?"

"O father," cried Walter; "when I saw what they were doing, I could not help contrasting this city with Boston, and this field with Boston Common."

"What were the points of contrast?"

"Why, here the Sabbath is being desecrated, while, probably, under a tent on Boston Common, some minister is preaching."

"Hity, tity, preaching on the Common!" shouted Minnie.

"Yes, there is preaching on the Common."

"I don't think so; there is in the churches."

"A religious association of young men have meetings there — don't they, pa?"

"I believe they do."

"Well, that makes the contrast a wide one."

Just then a heavy clap of thunder broke above their heads, and admonished them that they should return at once to the hotel. But they were two miles away, and they soon found the rain beginning to fall.

"Here is a door open; let us go in and stay until the rain is over," said the little girl, going up to a building well lighted.

"I suppose it is a Catholic church," replied Walter, "and we cannot understand a word."

The gentlemen both laughed.

"That is a queer church, Walter," said Mr. Tenant.

"Queer?"

"Yes."

"What do you mean?"

"Archbishop Tillotson once said such churches as that were the devil's chapels."

"What do you mean?"

"Why, that is a theatre; I see now," said Walter to Minnie.

"A theatre open Sunday evening?"

"Why not, as well as all that you have seen out in the pleasure grounds?"

"Sure enough; let us go on."

But go as fast as they could, they did not reach the hotel until the rain was pouring down in torrents. Mr. Tenant had a new hat completely drenched, and the children were wet to the skin; and as they entered their rooms, Minnie said, "You look like drowned rats."

"What do you look like, sis?" asked Walter.

"Like a half drowned rat, I suppose."

The next week was spent in viewing the city, which to the stranger is a very fine one. They found the people courteous and pleasant, and Minnie changed her opinions of the Austrians very much. A single fact will illustrate this. One day Mr. Percy came in and said to Minnie, "My daughter, I have had an instance of courtesy to-day, such as we should hardly expect to meet with at home."

"What was it?"

"I wanted to find a banker with whom I had

some business. I was deceived by a resemblance in names, and called on the wrong man. He soon saw whom I wanted, and at once endeavored to direct me to his place of business. But I know so little of the German language that I could not understand him. This he saw, and calling a young man, one of his clerks, sent him with me to the place."

"How far was it?"

"About a mile."

"He was very kind."

"Certainly he was, and I mention the instance to show you that in this country, that you have considered so benighted, the people know what belongs to genuine politeness."

"Would an American banker have been likely to have done this for you?" asked Walter.

"No, a Wall Street man would have looked at my papers, and turned away, abruptly saying, 'He don't do business here.' If I had asked where the man could be found, he would, perhaps, have directed me; but this Austrian banker sent his clerk to show me the way, keeping him from his work nearly an hour."

"I shall think better of this people," answered the boy.

"So shall I," replied the girl.

One day they all went to see the emperor's palace;

and while in the yard the emperor and empress came out, and entered the carriage for a drive. Thus they had a good view of the youthful pair who fill the imperial throne, and who have so much trouble within the empire and without it. Neither of them was called handsome by Minnie, who claimed to be a judge of such matters; but both were intelligent, interesting persons. The emperor was in military costume, and the empress in showy silks. The people around stared on in a sort of stupid wonder, as the imperial pair rode away.

"I should not like to be in his boots," said Walter.

"Why not?" asked his sister.

"Because his throne is dreadfully insecure."

"And his funds dreadfully low," added Mr. Tenant.

"Well, if I was in the shoes of the empress, I think I would risk the consequences, especially if the office was without the encumbrance of the emperor," said Minnie.

A laugh greeted this remark; and engaged in pleasant conversation about the imperial family and the condition of the empire, they returned to the hotel.

Chapter VI.

THE WONDERFUL CAVE.

CONNECTING Vienna with Trieste is a most wonderful railroad. Winding over lofty ranges of mountains, with towns and villages in the valleys below, shooting through long, dark, wet tunnels, hewn out of the solid rocks, it is a wonder to every one who travels over it. This was the way our party took when leaving " the Emperor's City."

"Three hundred and sixty miles are before us," said Mr. Percy, as they took their seats in the cars, one morning.

"Minnie cannot ride so far all at once," replied Mr. Tenant.

"No, indeed."

"I think we had better break up the ride into three parts."

"So I was thinking."

"Then I would suggest that we ride to-day as far as Gloggnitz."

"Why stop there?"

"Because the cars stop there about the time that I think we shall get tired."

"So be it then."

When they reached Gloggnitz, they found it a small, mean Austrian town, and soon began to fear that they had made a bad choice. A miserable inn in the centre of the village provided very poor accommodations, and was surrounded by a set of brigandish-looking fellows, who appeared as if they were ready for any bad game. However, they were obliged to make the best of it, and so went in and called for supper, which after a long time came.

"What is the name of this hotel?" asked Minnie.

"I don't know," replied her brother.

He called a maid servant, and tried to ask her what the hotel was called, but could not make her understand what he wanted. So, leaving the table, he ran out, and looked up at the front of the wretched-looking building, but could find no name any where, and came in, declaring that the inn had no name.

"Let us christen it, Walter."

"Well, what shall we call it?"

"Hardscrabble."

"No, that would be too bad."

"Then call it Hungry Hollow."

"No, I don't like that."

"Well, then, find a name yourself."

"I'll name the hotel Bostonia."

"O, dear, that would be an insult to Boston."

"How?"

"To call this filthy, dangerous-looking hotel after the Athens of America!"

"Well, Bostonia it shall be."

"That is right, Walter; give the town a good name; it may bring up its fare," said Mr. Tenant.

After supper they went out and walked the whole length of the village, and wandered along at the base of a mountain, on the side of which was a picturesquely situated convent, whose evening bells echoed far and wide over the valley below. At night they fastened their doors and windows securely, but were not disturbed. The breakfast of the next morning was an improvement on the supper of the evening before; and when they left the town, it was with far better impressions than when they entered it.

They could not fail to admire the railway over which they passed. It is an extraordinary achievement. It would hardly be a greater exploit to build a railroad over the Rocky Mountains, and constant were the expressions of pleasure from the party. At one time they were dashing through a dark tunnel, hewn out of the stony heart of the mountain; then along the brink of precipices that made them shudder to look down; then winding around the crags at so sharp a curve as to make them cling to the sides of the car, in fear that they were going over. Walter noted that they went through several tunnels, and he inquired the length of them, and found them as follows:—

Length of tunnel at Kresnitz,	.	570	feet.
" " Trifair,	. .	414	"
" " St. Georgen,		744	"
" " Pollschach,		588	"
" " "		768	"
" " Kranchsfield,		2,100	"
" " Baden,	. .	516	"
" " Spital,	. .	4,518	"
		10,218	

The train leaps out of one of these tunnels, and the traveller finds himself transferred in a moment from midnight darkness to broad flashing daylight, until he almost begins to believe that the prince of darkness has had something to do with the construction of the wonderful line.

While they were wondering at the grandeur of the enterprise, they were startled by several sudden screams of the locomotive.

"What is it, father," cried Minnie, as she clung to Mr. Percy's arm.

"I don't know, my child."

Again the shrill whistle was heard. The passengers leaped to their feet. All knew if there was danger there, it might be fearful beyond description, and for a moment none knew what most to dread. Wives clung to their husbands, and children to their parents, and some even shrieked with fear. But soon the cars stopped, and they found that a little child had wandered from a distant cottage on the mountains, and had gone to sleep upon the track, with the iron rail for its pillow. The fearful locomotive with the greatest exertion was brought to a giant halt not more than six feet from the poor innocent little thing, who awoke on finding itself surrounded with strange people, and looked upon them with smiles, little knowing what a fearful death he had just escaped. Many of the passengers got out, and among them our party; and Minnie took off a coral chain from her own neck, and placed it on the neck of the child, as he was in the arms of his mother, who had come rushing in terror to the spot.

When they were all seated again, they found an English gentleman in their car, who at once entered into conversation with them.

"Where do you stop to-night?" he asked.

"Somewhere between here and Trieste," said Mr. Percy; "but where, we have not concluded."

"We thought," added Mr. Tenant, "that we should go until we were tired of riding, and then stop."

"You should not," said the gentleman, "pass down over this road without stopping at Adelsburg."

"What is there?"

"Do you not know?"

"No, sir."

"Why, there is a wonderful cave."

"A cave!"

"Yes, sir, a mammoth, subterranean cavern under a mountain, that every traveller should see."

"Do you stop there?"

"No, I go on to Trieste; but I would advise you to stop."

"O, do, pa," said Minnie, "I want to see the cave."

"So do I," said Walter.

"Then we will stop there," replied Mr. Percy.

They found the town an insignificant one, the hotel filthy and wretched, and concluded that it must be a very fine cavern that could compensate for such annoyances. But the reader of Walter's journal, which contained a description of the cavern, would suppose that he was well repaid. Under the appropriate head he wrote, —

"We visited Adelsburg for the purpose of seeing a splendid grotto in the mountain, about a mile from the town, said to be the grandest natural excavation in Europe, if not in the world. The Mammoth Cave in Kentucky may exceed this in extent, but it can hardly surpass it in grandeur and beauty. We penetrate the dark bowels of the mountains four miles, and pass from one wonderful hall to another, all filled with saline formations, rivalling the rainbow in the gorgeousness of tinting, excelling the manufactures of men in the delicacy of fabrics, and outmastering the artisans of civilization in the statuary which God himself has been setting up here for ages on ages past. It was a wonderful day that we spent down in the dark grotto, where the fish have no eyes, and the noise of earth does not penetrate. Here are cathedrals, palaces, and prisons, beneath the ground, where Solitude, on his crystal throne, sits an acknowledged sovereign."

But we must describe what they saw in that famous grotto, for the cavern was wonderful

An English officer and his wife, who were in the dreadful siege of Lucknow, a Spanish marquis on a visit to Austria, and our party, started early in the morning. A walk of a quarter of an hour brought them to the foot of the mountain. They were accompanied by five men who acted as guides. The grotto consists of a series of immense caves, stretching for miles under the mountains, and the whole forms one of the most wonderful natural excavations in the world. Every year new caverns are found, new passages discovered, leading into deeper and wilder scenes. The grotto, as Walter says, is not as extensive as the Mammoth Cave, but far more sublime and beautiful. The visitor walks down a long passage of about three hundred yards, and all at once finds himself in a magnificent room, with a spacious dome; all hung with glittering, many-colored, ever-varying stalactites and stalagmites. The stalactites are comprised of carbonate of lime. The water sifting through limestone, and dripping into the cavern below, petrifies, and forms into all kinds of beautiful features. Here, in one cavern, which, on account of its peculiar form, is called "The Cathedral," the formations are very beautiful. In one place the water, which has been dripping down and petrifying for ages, has formed a long row of most beautiful columns, which look as if they had been carved out of solid marble. Then there are arches regularly turned, as if done by a human hand. Then there are sheets of stone, like transparent drapery, hung all around, or beautiful pendants, like icicles, which hang over your head. The cavern is about as large as a grand cathedral, and by a winding flight of steps we ascended to the pulpit, formed of the stalactites, and very curious and beautiful in its construction. Over the pulpit is a vast stone sounding board, hung there by nature, weighing some tons, and seeming as if about to fall upon the heads of those below. The guides lighted up this cavern for them to see, and the effect was wonderful. The crystalline forms, the hanging icicles of stone, the pillars huge and massive, of all colors, shades, and hues, made them feel, as they stood there, as if they had never seen any thing so beautiful. Passing out of the cathedral, they went into a number of caverns, stretching for miles onward. One of these was called the Ball Room, and once a year the people from all the region round about come here to have a grand hop. The ball room is as large as the cathedral, but of different form, and has a noble stone floor. When lighted and filled with people, the spectacle must be wonderful. The few lights they had making an impression upon the mind that Walter said he should never forget. Then they came to a vast room several times as large as this church, called the Crucifixion Room. It is thus called because the water dripping down has made three crosses, with images upon them. The guides climbed up the rocky sides of the cavern, and put their torches behind the figures, and the party could hardly believe that they did not see three images carved out by human hands. They could see the crosses, the bodies, and the people below.

Then they entered the Prison; a room so called because here nature has formed cells, with bars and grates. The guides ran ahead of them, and diving into these cells before they arrived, were looking upon them as they entered. As they saw them looking through the bars, it was hard to believe they were not in some prison, deep under the earth, and that these men were not real criminals, trying to escape from their confinement.

And all through the series of caverns they saw wonderful things. Here the stone had formed a most beautiful Madonna and Child; there, was an altar with a white-robed nun kneeling before it. There were rows of men, looking, at a little distance, as if alive, and houses and churches in the distance. These stalactites are so nearly transparent that one can almost see through them, and all were so perfect that the beholder could hardly believe the human hand had not carved them.

Through the grotto flows a deep, dark river. No one knows whence it comes, what the name of the water is, or where it goes. We see the river dashing rapidly on, but cannot tell whence it cometh or whither it goeth. There are fish in the stream, a sort of an eel, but having no eyes. Indeed, in that dark cave they need none. Walter regarded the day spent in there, beneath the mountains, amid those saline formations, as one of the most wonderful of his whole tour.

The party left Adelsburg late in the afternoon for Trieste. On the way down, over the same wonderful railroad, they had an awful thunder storm. The clouds came up suddenly. They were high above the little villages that nestled in the valleys below. At times nothing could be seen in any direction. The lightning flashed above and beneath them, and sometimes seemed to envelop the cars in a sheet of flame. Rain and hail thundered on the tops of the hollow cars, and the engine went leaping like a mad demon into darkness. The effect was awfully sublime; and after seeing the storm rage half an hour, they shot out of it into glorious sunset, where it seemed as if no rain had fallen. And soon the party were at Trieste, the port from whence they were to proceed to Venice.

"This has been a wonderful day," said Walter, as they stood on the pier at Trieste.

"Charming!" responded Minnie.

"So you have said, children, a hundred times to-day," added Mr. Tenant.

"Don't you agree with us?" asked the lad.

"Yes, exactly; but we must be on board the steamer, or she will be off without us."

"All aboard!"

Chapter VII.

THE BRIDE OF THE SEA.

THE round red sun was just rising from his bed when the steamer in which our friends had embarked at Trieste approached the ancient city of Venice, which has well been denominated the "Queen of the Adriatic." Scarcely any thing could be more beautiful than the scene presented; and it was not long before the passengers were crowded together in the fore part of the vessel, looking upon the unique and singular display of palaces, churches, and towers, which seemed to rise from the bosom of the sea.

"Is Venice much like London or Paris, pa?" asked Minnie.

"No, my child."

"What is it like?"

"It is not like any city we have seen."

"How does it differ?"

"Why, the streets are all water, and the people go out to do their shopping and visiting in boats."

"Pshaw! you are funning."

"No, I am not."

"How can it be so?"

"I will tell you."

"All water, you say?"

"Yes."

"No carriage ways, and streets with teams?"

"No."

"I don't understand."

"I see you do not; but I can enlighten you. The city of Venice was built long ago by refugees from the main land, who fled to the reeds and marshes of the Rialto, and amid the little islands built their houses and prepared their homes. From the bosom of the wave rose up the great city, with its palaces, churches, and towers. At first it was a miserable place, but in time became one of the most famous cities in the world; the glory of Venetian arms was sounded from Constantinople to Jerusalem, and the richness of her commerce was the wonder of the Archipelago. From a little city of huts and rushes arose a great and magnificent republic, and in the sea appeared fine edifices, which far outshone those upon the solid land. Unlike any other city on earth, the seat of vast wealth, filled with a joyous and pleasure-loving people, it became, and continued for a while, the most gay and delightful city in the world, mocking even the splendors of Rome, Florence, and Ferrara. Artists and poets here gathered to kindle the sacred flame of art, and men of commerce here convened to amass princely fortunes. The lovers of the beautiful and the sublime, the priests of religion, the slaves of sensualism, all found in Venice congenial pursuits and associates; and, up to this hour, the city is the resort of travellers from all parts of the world."

"It must be a wonderful city."

"It is. It is built upon seventy-two islands, and is connected by three hundred and six bridges, scarcely any of which can be crossed by a carriage."

"O, how funny!"

"If we had arrived by land instead of by steamer, we ——"

"I thought you said there was no land."

"The city is connected with the main land by a long stone railway bridge, and travellers arriving by railway, instead of cabs and carriages such as we see in France and England, find a long line of neat gondolas, each manned, and ready to put off into the city."

The steamer was now near the city, and surrounded by boatmen in their gondolas, all of whom were clamorous to take the passengers to the shore. The party entered one of the boats, and were soon gliding swiftly towards the shore. Walter noticed that the boatman, by a skilful use of his oar, was enabled to urge his boat forward with great speed. As they moved on, Minnie turned to her brother, and said, —

"Walter!"

"What, sis?"

"What do you call this craft — a *droskie*, hey?"

"A gondola."

"A pretty name."

"Yes, and a pretty craft, as you will see by looking at that one over there," said Walter, pointing to a beautiful boat near them.

The gondola is a long boat, with very sharp bows and stern. A pavilion for passengers is in the middle of the boat, and one or two men manage the craft with ease.

"They are all black, Walter!"

"I see they are. Father tells me that a long time ago the most fantastic colors and decorations were used, and the greatest extravagance, on the part of the boatmen, ensued; and a law was made prohibiting any other color than that you see."

"I should not think government would interfere with these little boats."

"It does, just as the city government of

Boston regulates the coaches that run from the depots. These gondolas have an admirable system, if the accounts I have read are true. The fares, the number of passengers, and the amount of baggage to be carried, are all regulated by government, and each gondolier carries his tariff of prices in his pocket, or in the saloon of his little vessel."

The boat now touched the landing; and a number of porters, taking their baggage on their shoulders, marched off with it to a hotel in the grand square of San Marco. And now commenced with our travellers a most delightful week of day dreaming; for few persons are conscious of being fully awake in this enchanting city.

The morning following the arrival of the party, Minnie awoke early, and the first sounds she heard, after opening her eyes, were the sweet notes of a Venetian song. At first, the little girl thought the singer was in the house, but as she listened, the sounds seemed wafted up from below. She ran to the window, and on looking out saw in the canal below a gondola filled with flowers and fruit. One part of the boat was like a mammoth bouquet, and the air around seemed filled with sweet odors; another part of the boat was devoted to fruit, and most tempting was the display made; and still another part of the boat was laden with vegetables, just taken from the earth; and in the midst of the whole, like a fairy, was a young girl, with a neat white cap upon her head, singing a most captivating song, in the pleasant, flowing accents of Italy.

"Charming! charming! I should like to live here always," said Minnie to herself.

"What, in this pond?" asked her brother, who had entered unperceived.

"Pond! call this a pond! Why, I am charmed with the city, before I have seen it."

"Well, cease your admiration, and bid adieu to your romantic ideas, and come to breakfast. We have been waiting for you some time;" and the lad tripped away, repeating to himself, —

> "Underneath day's azure eyes,
> Ocean's nursling, Venice, lies —
> A peopled labyrinth of walls,
> Amphitrite's destined halls,
> Which her hoary sire now paves
> With his blue and beaming waves."

After breakfast the party prepared to go out and see the place; but Minnie did not understand how they were to see much if there were no carriages to ride in. Crossing the square they entered the cathedral of San Marco, a very noted edifice. As they crossed the threshold

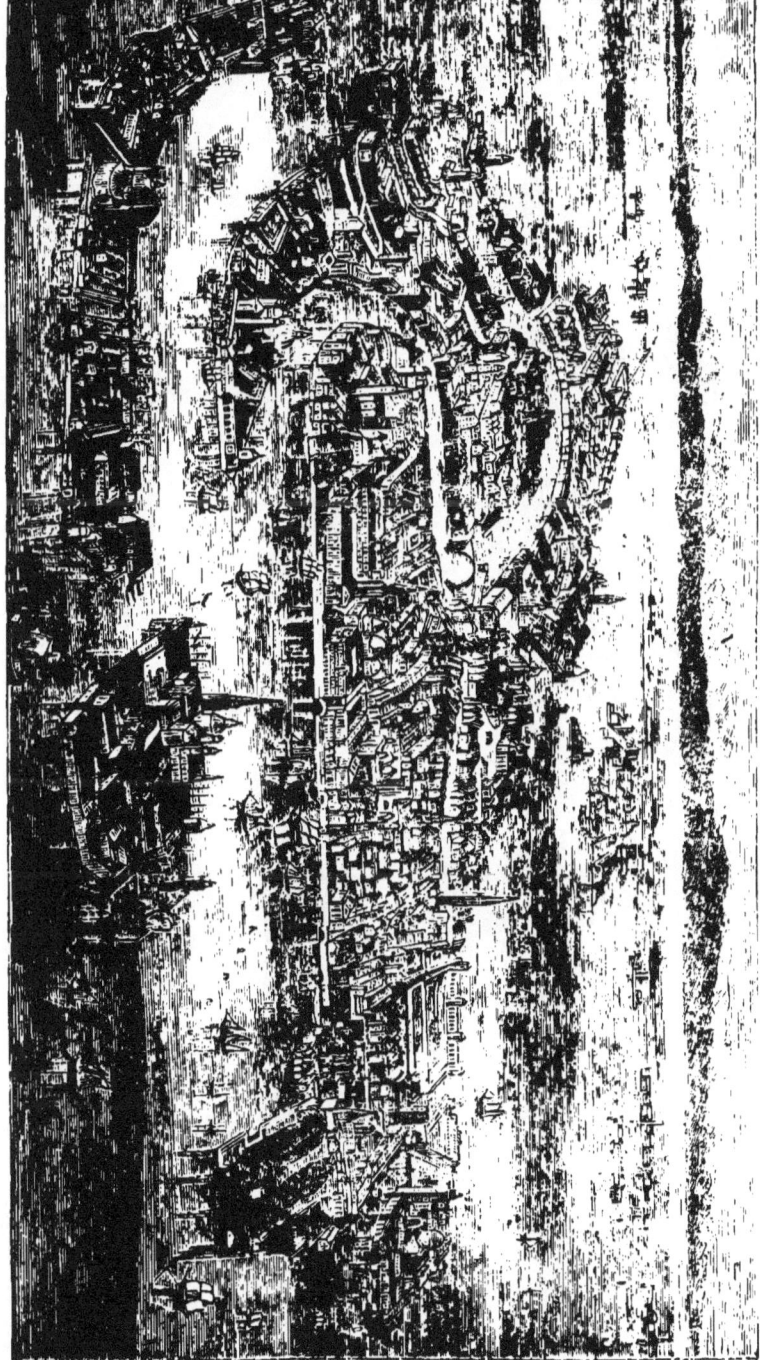

VENICE.

Mr. Percy pointed to a piece of colored marble set in the pavement, and told them that there an arrogant pope set his foot upon the neck of the Emperor Frederick Barbarossa, who knelt to do him homage, saying as he did so, "Thus I tread upon the pride of kings." They found the cathedral unlike any other building they had seen. Walter was very much interested; but Minnie declared that she did not care any thing about the curious architecture. She was most interested in the service which was going on, and the robes of the priests, which were very gaudy and showy.

From the church they went to the campanile, or bell tower, a large square column, and over winding stairs they arrived to the top, and sat down among the bells. The view from the tower is very fine, and they enjoyed it for a long time.

The next visit was to the doge's palace, and to the old prisons, which they reached over the famous Bridge of Sighs. The dungeons were dark and loathsome, and the children trembled as they entered them. They also saw instruments of torture that were used in past times; and as they looked upon them, Mr. Tenant related several tales of barbarity perpetrated in this prison, until Minnie asked him to lead her out into daylight.

In the afternoon, they took a gondola and went out to visit some public buildings. They saw an elegant church rising out of the water, and on entering found it filled with beautiful paintings and exquisitely carved statues. Minnie caught a large shell-fish on the steps as she came out, which she held up, shouting, " Here is a crab on his way to church."

" He will get as much benefit as my little wild-brained sister," replied Walter.

" It is very saucy in you to tell ―― "

The reply of Minnie was broken off by an unexpected occurrence, and she finished with a cry of pain, ―

" O, O, O, dear me!"

" What is the matter? " asked Mr. Percy, turning back.

" O, dear! take him off, take him off."

The cause of the trouble was soon ascertained. The crab had taken one of the little girl's fingers into his open claw, and it was with some difficulty that he was forced to relinquish his hold. Throwing the fish into the water, Mr. Percy helped his daughter into the boat, where she hid her face for a while behind the drapery of the pavilion, watching through the folds the faces of her friends.

" Father," at length she exclaimed.

"What, my child?"

"Walter is making fun of me."

"How, my dear?"

"Why, I see by his face that he is glad that that ugly creature bit me."

Walter laughed; and to tell the truth, as Minnie was not much hurt, he was glad of it, as it gave him an opportunity to plague her a little. Very soon, however, all this was forgotten in the enjoyment they experienced in passing along the narrow canals, gliding beneath the bridges, or looking upon the stately palaces, once so full of mirth, now almost deserted, and going to decay. They sailed the whole length of the Rialto or main canal, which runs through the city nearly in the form of an inverted *S*.

"I don't see," said Walter, "how the people live here. There are no lands to cultivate, no public manufactures, none of the usual means of obtaining a livelihood. I do not see how the people live."

"And I," said Minnie, "do not see where the children play. I should think they would always be getting into the canals and drowned."

"People can get used to every thing," answered Mr. Tenant. "The children get accustomed to boats just as the children at home get accustomed to horses and carriages. Besides, they can play at home, and in some of the streets that are not composed of water. And if Walter lived here, he would find no trouble in getting a living. It does not cost much to live here, and the people are employed in the manufacture of articles that do not require extensive warehouses. These old palaces are occupied by people of wealth from other lands, who have rented them for a longer or shorter period, and the means of living are as —— "

Crash, crash, crash!

"Look out there, boatman!" Mr. Percy was heard shouting.

"O, dear me!" cried Minnie.

"Take care," shouted Walter.

"Danger over," said Mr. Tenant, whose remarks were cut short by the violent contact of another boat with that in which our party were sailing. The boatmen of the two gondolas now began reproaching each other, gesticulating very violently, and for a time it seemed as if a serious difficulty was liable to occur; but Mr. Tenant, with a great deal of firmness, took his own gondolier by the arm and ordered him to proceed, which, with many smothered curses, he did.

Our party remained in Venice a week. The days were spent mostly in the galleries of art, and the evenings in roaming over the waters, along the canals, and sometimes out miles into the Adriatic. The evening entertainment was very novel, and pleased Minnie very much; and she often declared, as she floated out at night, she could not make the city appear like a reality. The gondolas lighted with lanterns of many colors, the pavilions filled with gay, happy men and women, whose songs echoed far and wide over the waves, made the whole seem like enchantment, rather than reality.

Chapter VIII.

CITY OF ARTISTS AND FLOWER GIRLS.

"IT is so curious," said Minnie, as she stepped into a gondola.

"What is so curious?" asked Walter.

"Why, to take a boat to go to the railroad depot."

"It is funny. When I went to the hotel keeper and asked him about the best ways of getting to the depot, he told me that the omnibus would start in season to get us there, and that it would take us at lower fare than we could get carried for otherwise."

"Omnibus, did he say?"

"Yes."

"Well, where is it?"

"He meant the boat we are in."

"A pretty omnibus, truly!"

But it took our travellers to the station, and they were soon on board the cars for Verona, at which place they arrived at midnight. They rode a long distance in an omnibus, and reached a hotel, and after a great deal of knocking and thumping to arouse the inmates, at length a porter appeared and let them in, grumbling and scolding that he should be called up at so late an hour.

There is not much to amuse the stranger in Verona, and our friends saw all they wished to in a single day. Walter was interested in the ruins of a noble amphitheatre, with its stone steps rising one upon another, sufficient to seat twenty thousand persons.

"What did they use this amphitheatre for?" he asked of his father.

"Probably for gladiatorial exhibitions; and the pavement you see before you was doubtless often wet with blood."

"With human blood?"

"Most likely."

"Was it not very cruel in the ancients to make men fight with wild beasts?"

"Certainly it was; and we may be thankful to God that these days have gone by."

"How did they get the beasts into the vacant spot? What do you call it?" asked Minnie.

"The arena."

"Yes."

"I will show you," replied Mr. Percy; and he took the children down into the cells under the walls, where were doors and gates leading into the arena, and dungeons for prisoners, and strong apartments for the bloody monsters who, goaded to madness by hunger, were ready to tear the flesh of their victims.

"This structure," said the father to his children, "gives you a very fine idea of the mammoth amphitheatres erected by the ancients for theatrical and gladiatorial purposes."

"Shall we see any other besides this?" asked Walter.

"O, yes; you know we shall see the Colosseum at Rome, which is larger and grander than this. We shall also see one or two others; but what state of preservation they are in, I cannot tell."

"There is one thing we must see while we are here," said Mr. Tenant, as they entered the carriage.

"What is it?" asked the children in one breath.

"The tomb of Juliet."

"Who was she?" asked Minnie.

"One of Shakspeare's characters, about whom Walter will tell you."

"Driver," said he to that personage, "do you know where the tomb of Juliet is?"

The driver shook his head.

"The tomb of Juliet," repeated Mr. Tenant.

"No comprehend," was all the answer that could be obtained.

The information was found elsewhere, and the party were soon carried to what purports to be the tomb of the heroine. They entered a narrow passage, in which a man was washing the dirty wheels of a carriage, and where were several horses, which nearly trampled them as they passed on, and knocked at a rude door, which was opened by a woman with a child in her arms. She was an Italian woman, with a dark skin, coal-black eyes, piercing and glistening, and a form as graceful as a sibyl. Giving her babe to another, she conducted them through a stable into a garden. They passed along under a heavy overhanging grape vine, well hung with unripe fruit, to a little chapel, once used for devotional purposes, and in which a tolerable fresco of the crucifixion still remains. Here, in this chapel, which is now used for dovecot and hencoop, a stone tub was pointed out as the veritable coffin of Juliet. The hole left as a breathing place was pointed out. Visitors have broken off pieces of the marble, and carried it away.

"Do you believe that this is the tomb of Juliet?" asked Minnie of her father.

"No."

"Do you believe there ever was a real Juliet?" asked Walter.

"No; but it answers the same purpose to give these poor people a few pence for opening the gate."

"I must get a piece of this stone tub," said Walter to himself, as he took up a stone to break off a piece.

"Ah, no! no!! no!!!" cried the woman.

Walter pulled out his purse and offered her money. He had found, almost every where, that a golden bribe would soften the heart of almost any official character, and he supposed this woman would yield at once. But she was inexorable.

"No possible — no possible!" she said.

He then tried to coax her a little, and with fair compliments secure a piece of the marble; but though her reply to his persuasions was less indignant than before, it was no less firmly given: —

"No possible — no possible!"

Having "done up Verona," as Walter said, they then went back some miles to a station on the railroad by which they came, and took a diligence for Florence.

"What is a diligence?" asked Minnie, while on her way to the booking office.

"A sort of stage or omnibus, in which the

people of this country, where railroads are few, usually travel," replied her father.

As the young reader has never seen a diligence, a description of one may not be uninteresting, and we give it in nearly the words we find in Walter's journal. He there says, "The diligence itself is a long, cumbersome vehicle, like an omnibus, and would not be tolerated in Yankeeland a half hour. It is divided into different compartments. The cabriolet is an open sort of a chaise on top; the *coupé* is the forward apartment, will hold four or five persons, and is considered as the best place for observation and ease; the *interno*, or interior, is an apartment with two seats opposite, like those in a coach, and is in the middle; while below is the *rotunda*, with two seats opposite, on the sides, like those of an omnibus. These seats will hold two, three, or four persons, according to the size of the vehicle. The baggage is put upon the top of the crazy carriage, and is liable every moment to fall through on to your head."

" Mercy! have we got to ride in that?" cried Minnie, as she saw it.

" Yes; why not, sis?" asked her brother.

" It will break down."

" I guess not."

" It looks like an ox team; what did you call it?"

"A diligence!"

"You will find that thing to be a *dilatory*, I tell you."

A man now led forward four horses, at which Minnie exclaimed, "See those skeletons that are to draw us."

"Skeletons?"

"Yes; those four horses, as lean and lank as Pharaoh's lean kine, and as hungry, too. And the harness is partly of leather, and partly of rope, rotten as twine, and as clumsy as a bed cord."

"You are sarcastic, sis."

"Who could help being, at such a contrivance as this?"

"You had better wait, and see what kind of riding the diligence gives us."

"The *dilatory*, you mean!"

The gentlemen had been engaged a moment in looking about for their baggage, when they heard Minnie call to Walter.

"Bub! bub! look at that funny little chap."

"Where?"

"Standing in the doorway of the office."

Walter looked, and saw a small man, with a patent leather hat, with a steeple crown, on his head, an old-fashioned faded military coat on his back, a tin horn under one arm, and a monstrous whip in his hand.

"Who is he, Walter?"

"I don't know."

"Who do you take him to be?"

"I take him to be the Napoleon of this vehicle."

"Hum! satisfactory answer, I think."

Then, turning to Mr. Tenant, she asked, —

"Who is that pompous little fellow, with a military coat on, standing like a major on the steps?"

"O, that is the postilion," replied the gentleman.

"And what does he do?"

"He rides the forward horse."

"What for?"

"O, it is the custom."

The horses were harnessed, and the diligence all ready. It was arranged that Mr. Tenant and Walter should occupy the cabriolet, while Mr. Percy and his daughter took the coupé. And so they journeyed on, about six miles an hour, for two or three days, stopping on the way to see the places of interest. Among these were Ferrara and Bologna. In the former place they saw the prison of Tasso, a little cell twenty feet long and ten feet wide, where he was imprisoned by the duke for aspiring to the hand of his sister, the beautiful Eleanora; and on the wall Walter found the name of Byron, engraved there by himself. Mr. Percy told the children who Tasso was, and Mr. Tenant repeated those touching lines of his, written while imprisoned by the cruel Alphonso, in which he asks, —

> "Am I, a living, breathing corpse, interred,
> To go not forth till prisoned in my bier?"

They also went to the house of Ariosto, in which they found his room just as he left it. The chair on which he sat, the table at which he wrote, and the very inkstand which he used remain. His tomb is in the Church of the Benedictines, and over it yet stands the lightning-riven bust, and is visited by many who have read and admired his writings.

At Bologna, which Walter called the "Sausage City," they saw two leaning towers. They are huge rude columns; the highest rises three hundred and sixteen feet, and inclines several feet. This inclination was caused by the settling of the ground in time of an earthquake. In one of the churches they found the tomb of St. Dominic, the founder of the Inquisition, who sleeps here, while the world curses his memory; also the tomb of the great painter Guido, and several others of much eminence.

At length they arrived at Florence, and were

driven through streets crowded with people and decked with flowers, to the hotel.

"We are fortunate," said Mr. Tenant, a few minutes after their arrival.

"Why so?" asked Mr. Percy, who was unstrapping his trunk.

"Because this is San Victoria's day, and great celebrations are taking place. So the keeper of the house tells me."

"That is good," cried Minnie. "I have been cooped up in the *dilatory* so long that I want some fun."

"You don't know as you will get it," answered her brother.

"What is the fun to consist of, Mr. Tenant?" queried Minnie.

"They have some ceremonies all day, and we have reached here in season to see the finale."

"And what is that?"

"A horse-race."

"Pho! I don't want to see that."

"Don't?"

"No, I am sure I don't."

"It is not such a sort of horse-races as you have heard of."

"Is there more than one kind of horse-race?"

"There seems to be a new kind here."

"What is it?"

"Three horses are painted and lettered, and let loose in the public streets. So they tell me."

"Nonsense."

"Perhaps so; yet that is the sport of this afternoon."

An hour or two after the people began to assemble, and soon crowded the thoroughfares and windows all along the race course by thousands; military men were parading up and down; and for two hours the children gazed from the window of the hotel upon an array of beauty, fashion, pride, pomp, and vanity such as they had never seen before. The houses all along were waving with drapery, which was suspended from the windows, and every thing gave evidence that some gay event was about to transpire.

"I wish they would come," cried Minnie.

"So do I," answered Walter.

At length a cry was heard, the people fell back on both sides, and soon the horses came on,— the little creatures all spotted with paint,—and in a moment were out of sight. From the window of the hotel they looked much like large wharf rats leaping by, and sending their heels into the faces of the crowds of people who lined the streets on both sides.

"Well, Min, what do you think of that?" asked Mr. Tenant.

ARTISTS AND FLOWER GIRLS. 111

"It is a humbug."

"It reminds me," said Walter, "of the exhibition of 'three blind mice.'"

The next day they went out, and no city, since leaving Paris, pleased Minnie so much as this. She was particularly pleased with the flower girls, whose arms were full of beautiful bouquets, which they were ready to sell for whatever any one would pay for them.

Walter was very anxious to see the artists, and he persuaded the gentlemen to take him again and again to the studios. He seemed to feel an awe as he entered the little apartment where Powers modelled Eve and the Greek Slave, and where his workmen were still engaged on marble forms that were constantly developing new beauties. At Greenough's he met several American gentlemen, who answered many questions in relation to sculpture and other branches of art. One day, when he came home from the studio of Pampaloni, whither he had gone alone, he said to Minnie, —

"Don't you remember a plaster image over the library in our Sunday school?"

"Yes."

"What is it?"

"You know."

"Well, do you know?"

"Yes, it is little Samuel kneeling in prayer."

"You know they are very common."

"Yes, almost every Italian image seller has them. But what of it?"

"Just this — I have seen the original. Pampaloni, to whose studio I have been, designed that, cast it in plaster, and then carved it in marble."

"And all that we see are copies."

"Yes."

"Did you see Pampaloni, who made it?"

"No, he is dead; but his son inherits his genius."

One day they rode out, and as they went, Mr. Tenant directed the driver to take them to Santa Croce.

"Santa Croce!" said Minnie; "what is that?"

"A church, Min," said Walter.

"A church, hey?"

"Yes; Santa Croce, erected six hundred years ago, is to Florence what Westminster Abbey is to London — the charnel of its illustrious dead. So I read in the guide books."

When they reached the edifice, they found it filled with many monuments, among which is, in a most conspicuous position, the grand sarcophagus of Michael Angelo, the world's great artist. The sister arts, Painting, Sculpture, and

THE CAMPANILE, FLORENCE.

Architecture, are weeping over the tomb, while surmounting them is a statue of the great man himself. The spot where he sleeps was selected, and the manner of his burial was described, by the artist himself, who wished his resting place to be within sight of the cathedral, on whose spacious dome he loved to gaze in life. They also saw the monuments of Dante, Alfieri, and Galileo.

It would take a long time to tell all the children saw in Florence, or *Firenze*, as the Italians spell it. One or two funeral processions they met in the street, one or two masses they saw solemnized in the churches, visits they made to the cathedral, many times they climbed up into the bell tower, excursions they took out into the country, and so much pleasure did they secure, that Minnie declared she could not tell which city she liked best, Florence or Paris. Walter thought that when he became a man, and had money of his own to spend, and time enough at his command, he would come and live a year in Florence.

So it is, that we often make plans in childhood that are never realized in manhood; we anticipate pleasures that we never secure. With this reflection we leave Walter dreaming in the city of flower girls and artists.

Chapter IX.

FIRST VIEWS OF ROME.

AS the lumbering diligence rolled towards Rome, the interest of the party increased. Minnie, who had her seat in the coupé, often called to her brother,—

"Walter, do you see any thing?"

"Not yet," was his reply as often to her impatient questions. Still the vehicle rolled heavily onward, the cracking whip was heard, and the eager expectation of the company manifested itself in vain endeavors to catch some outline of the Eternal City.

"There it is!" at length Walter exclaimed, and looking forward they all saw the dome of St. Peter's, like a huge bank resting against the sky. The interest was now most lively, and as the distance to the city was diminished every minute, all feeling of fatigue, and all sense of weariness were forgotten, and soon they were beneath the walls. After an examination by custom-house officials, they passed through the Porta Cavalleggieri,—where the French suffered so dreadfully in their attack on the city several years ago, and at which they entered with the most terrible loss, — leaving St. Peter's to the left, rolling down the hill, across the Pons Ælius, under the very shadow of the Castle of St. Angelo, over which the Roman flag was flying, but beneath which French soldiers were leaning on their arms, the masters of the city, and the rulers of the pope himself.

And from that time commenced a most pleasant residence in Rome, which was protracted to months, all of which were filled up with interest and profit.

"I have heard," said Walter, one day, "Rome called the 'City of Seven Hills.' Why is that?"

"Because," replied his father, "Rome is located in the midst of the great Roman Campagna, on seven hills. The Tiber divides it, and flows in its sluggish course through its very midst. The best view is obtained from the tower of the Capitol, on the Capitoline Hill, from which the other six, the Quirinal, the Viminal, the Palatine, the Aventine, the Esquiline, and the Cælian, are all in view."

"How many inhabitants are there in Rome?"

"The number of inhabitants at the present time is only one hundred and fifty thousand, or less than the number of the inhabitants of Boston.

Of this limited number, some fifty or sixty are cardinals, twenty-three are bishops, sixteen hundred and thirty-nine are priests, twenty-six hundred and twelve are monks, fifteen hundred and fifty are nuns, and eight thousand are Jews, who live in a quarter of the city appropriated to themselves."

"What is the government? Who is the head?"

"The government is a medley of religion and politics, the pope being alike at the head of church and state."

"You have often told us of the view obtained of the city from the Capitol — can we not go and get that view soon?"

"Yes, to-day, if Mr. Tenant finds it convenient."

That gentleman, on being consulted, declared that nothing could please him better; and so it was resolved to visit the Capitol. They took a carriage, and employed a *valet de place* to point out to them the objects of interest. They soon arrived, and passing up the hill, by the old mile post of Vespasian, Mr. Percy pointed out to his children the bronze horse, — from which, on festive occasions long agone, water ran from one nostril and wine from the other, — and various other statues of merit and celebrity, in all of

FIRST VIEW OF ROME. 119

which they were much interested. When they entered the building, which is a very fine one, they saw many things which pleased them.

"See that iron cat," said Minnie.

"Where?" asked her brother.

"There!" she said, pointing to a metallic beast which seemed to draw much attention.

"I know what that is," replied Walter.

"What is it?"

"It is the famous bronze wolf;" and then the kind-hearted little lad told his sister the story of Romulus, the founder of the city, who, when deserted by natural parents, was suckled by a wolf.

"And what is that?" she asked, pointing to the statue of the dying gladiator.

Walter told her, and repeated some lines he had committed to memory, written in description of this remarkable work of art, and Minnie declared them wonderfully just.

When they had seen the inside of the edifice, they went up to the top of the tower, which is surmounted by a colossal image holding a cross. Walter climbed up, and stood where few persons stand, holding himself by the cross. From this high point the view was a fine one, and for hours they enjoyed it.

"Now, pa," said Minnie, "describe the various objects, point out the localities, that we may fix them in our minds."

Walter came down from his high and somewhat dangerous elevation, and sat down at his father's feet, while the little girl stood looking into his face as he made the following statement: —

"The Capitol seems to divide what are called the old and the new cities. We look out from the elevation in one direction, and at our feet is the old Roman Forum, stretching away from the slope of the hill to the Palatine; conspicuously in front are the ruins of the old Temple of Saturn and the House of Concord; the Arch of Septimius Severus, in a good state of preservation, and covered with bass-reliefs;

'The nameless column, with a buried base;'

the pillars of the Temples of Minerva and Romulus; the winding Via Sacra, the favorite walk of Horace, the world-renowned Way, trod by emperors, warriors, and priests; the old Coliseum, looking like some gigantic citadel, covered with the moss of ages, and gazing down with frowns upon the surrounding city; the Arch of Titus, with bass-reliefs representing the conqueror's return from Jerusalem, bringing with him the consecrated vessels of the Jewish temple;

and numberless other relics of the dead and buried past."

These various objects Mr. Percy pointed out, giving historical facts calculated to fix in the minds of the children what they had seen.

"You spoke," said Minnie, of 'a nameless column, with a buried base'!"

"Yes."

"What did you mean by that?"

"The quotation is from Byron, who thus speaks of a beautiful column which you see yonder. The base is buried, and it was not known when he wrote what it was erected for, or what name it bore."

"Is it now known?"

"Yes; since he wrote, the history of the pillar has been discovered, and when we descend I will tell you all that is known about it."

"Now, father, what do we see in the other direction?"

"There the new city lies before you."

"Yes."

"You see the Corso."

"What is that?"

"The long street you see filled with people."

"What else?"

"Why, the River Tiber, winding its way upon its noiseless course; the domes of churches and the roofs of convents; and, back of all, the form of St. Peter's, rising in its vast proportions and beautiful architecture, while all around is stretched the desolate Campagna, like a plain of death, thick with malaria and contagion."

"And I," said Walter, "have been looking over to the distant mountains, whose sides are adorned with villas, vineyards, and tombs."

"Ah, Walter, you never expected to witness this grand spectacle," remarked Mr. Tenant.

"No, sir, indeed I did not; and it seems hardly real that I can be in Rome now, and on the top of the Capitol. It seems like a dream; and ever since I have been here I have been saying to myself, —

> ' Ah, little thought I, when in school I sat,
> A schoolboy on his bench, in early dawn,
> Glowing with Roman story, I should live
> To tread the Appian . . . .
>   . . . . or climb the Palatine,
> Long while the seat of Rome!' "

"Bah! what are you but a schoolboy now?" cried Minnie, who had been looking in another direction.

"What a plague you are, Min!"

"How do I plague you?"

"Why, I cannot quote a line of poetry, or do any thing else, but you have something to say."

"What was my tongue given me for?"

"Not to ridicule."

"Well, never mind, Walter, I'll stop."

"Until next time!" slyly suggested Mr. Tenant.

It would take much time to tell all our travellers saw, and where they went that winter. Walter wrote home to his mother that they had seen acres of pictures, continents of churches, armies of beggars, and swarms of monks. He gave her a particular description of some of the churches; among the rest, St. John Lateran, which, he told her, was the first Christian church, built by Constantine in the fourth century. He told her, what may well be doubted, that the emperor, day after day, until it was finished, worked on it with his own hands like a slave. He also described the baptistery in which Rienzi bathed, on the night before his death, to show his contempt of sacred things.

Walter also sent to Charlie a description of one church he saw, which the little fellow took all over the neighborhood and read to his young friends. This church, he wrote to his brother, has deep vaults which are filled up as a burial ground. The earth in it was brought from Jerusalem, and is held sacred by the monks. The vaults consist of an aisle and six little chapels, or niches, about ten feet wide, eight feet high, and six feet deep. These chapels are arched, and resemble niches in a wall. When a monk dies, he is buried here, and is allowed to rest beneath the ground a while, when he is unburied, clad in the very same habit which he wore in life, and laid out in state a while, when the bones are taken to pieces and scraped. They are then piled up in fantastic order. These vaults, on entering them, have a most singular effect. The arches are all lined with bones; skulls are laid up in piles; while the small bones are formed into crosses on the walls, and even the chandeliers in which hang the lamps which illuminate the aisle are of parts of the human body, tastefully framed together. Skeletons sit astride piles of skulls, or hang suspended from the wall, while hands and feet, long and bony, reach out in every direction.

It seemed as if Walter never would tire of seeing the ancient buildings, that link this with a former age. One day the party all visited the Pantheon.

"What did you come to this old place for?" asked Minnie.

"Because it is an old place," answered Walter.

"If you had an eye to architectural beauties

you would not ask the question, my child," said Mr. Percy.

"How old is this church — a thousand years?" asked Minnie.

"Yes, more than that," replied her father.

"When was it built?"

"Twenty-six years before Christ."

"Is it possible?"

"Not only possible, but certain."

"Built before the angels sang on the plains of Bethlehem," said Minnie to herself.

"Yes," replied her father; "it is the oldest building, in a state of preservation, in the world. Some of the old ruins of Rome date farther back than this. But they are fallen, and have become a pile of ruins. But this stands, and I see no reason why it may not stand eighteen hundred years longer."

Several other ancient edifices, still in a state of preservation, were seen, each with a long and eventful history. The children became acquainted with two Capuchin monks, who, having time to spare, took them to many places that otherwise would have been overlooked. Mr. Percy allowed them sometimes, in company with himself or Mr. Tenant, to visit the monks at their convent; but both of them were so much disgusted with the cloisters that they did not wish to go often. Walter described the monks, in a letter to friends at home, to be a most self-denying class. He wrote that their cells are about six feet square. The monk sleeps on a hard board; no bed, no mattress; a single woollen covering only keeping the rough wood from a contact with the body of the sleeper. A rough table, a bench, or chair, compose the furniture of the room. To quote his own words, "We saw one day on the table, in the cell of Father Francis, or Giacomo Foscari, as his real name was, a loaf of bread, some burnt coffee, and, on a little shelf, a few books. The friars of this order wear a woollen habit, no stockings, vest, nor under clothing of any description. They eat little meat, and live by charity, and their reputation for sanctity is very high. They are of all ages, from the young man just entering life to the old man in his dotage." Walter could not endure the idea that while millions of money were expended on churches, these monks should have such scanty fare, and live in such poverty.

Chapter X.

PILGRIMAGE TO ST. PETER'S.

ALMOST the first place the stranger visits in Rome is the Cathedral of St. Peter. That huge edifice seems to be the centre of attraction. The art-glories of the Vatican, the memorials of fallen pride that gather in the Roman Forum, the sovereign pontiff himself, are not so remarkable as the grand pile in which the religion of half the civilized world is enshrined.

"To-day we go to St. Peter's," said Walter to his sister, one morning as they were waiting on the steps of the hotel for the gentlemen who were somewhat tardy in making their appearance.

"Good; I wonder we have not gone there before."

"I wish father would come."

"I am coming," said Mr. Percy, making his appearance, and soon after Mr. Tenant was on hand.

They walked slowly towards the Cathedral; and as they passed from street to street, the conversation turned upon the edifice they were about to visit.

"Father," said Walter, "can you tell me any thing about St. Peter's."

"Any thing about it! What do you mean?"

"Yes, about its origin and history."

"Ah, yes."

"Then you will find me a listener."

"As to the origin of the Cathedral, I can soon tell you all I know. It is *supposed* to stand on or near the spot where the apostle, for whom it is named, was buried."

"Supposed?"

"Yes; for many have doubted whether Peter ever was at Rome."

"Is there no way of finding out?"

"I know of none. All these things are matters of very vague and indefinite tradition."

"Well, what about the erection of the church?"

"It was at first an insignificant little chapel, which had more the appearance of a tomb than a temple. In the time of Constantine, this little structure was removed, and a fine church built on the spot, which, in its turn, gave place to the magnificent Cathedral."

"Do you know what it cost, and how long it took to finish it?"

"It required more than three centuries to complete it; forty-three popes gave it their time and attention, and when finished, seventy millions of dollars had been expended upon it. It covers between five and six acres, and is kept in repair at an expense of about thirty thousand dollars annually."

"Walter," asked Minnie, "how many square feet are there in the number of acres father named?"

"About two hundred and forty thousand square feet, as near as I can calculate."

The young reader will figure it out, and see how near Walter came to it.

The party now approached the edifice, and stood looking upon its noble exterior.

The best idea of the building will be obtained if you imagine an immense circular area enclosed with the finest colonnade in the world, the front open, and the rear filled up by the Cathedral. In this area two fine fountains are ever playing, and between them a column, surmounted by a cross, rises to the height of a hundred feet. The colonnades are formed by two hundred and eighty-four columns, sixty feet high, covered with spacious galleries. These form a magnificent entrance to the church, bending around the visitor as he advances, impressing him with an idea of strength and dignity. The front of the church is somewhat marred by a façade, which hides the proportions of the building, and but poorly compares with the architectural design of the monstrous dome. Passing between marble figures of Peter and Paul, we enter the church, and pause, almost overpowered with the effect produced. The colossal statues, the vaulted roof, the spacious aisles, the hurrying priests, and the wonderful dome, all produce in the mind a feeling of awful sublimity.

The first emotion of awe being over, our party began to look about. They found the service being performed in different parts of the building, in different dialects; they saw multitudes of men and women walking about or kneeling on the floor; they saw the grand altar, beneath the dome, and heard the music from sounding organs and harmonious choirs.

As they walked about, Walter asked, " What image is that? "

They all looked, and Minnie cried out, —

" I declare ! "

" You do ! what do you declare ? " asked her father.

" Why, they are kissing it ! "

" So they are," said Walter.

" What is it, pa ? "

"It is a bronze statue that is here reverenced as that of Peter."

"Where did it come from?"

"It was found among the ruins of old Rome, and is supposed to have been an image of Jupiter. One of the popes put it here, and thousands come and offer it their homage."

They walked up to it, and found the great toe of one foot, which was extended, worn down flat.

"What has done that?" Minnie asked.

"It has been kissed away."

"Kissed away?" queried Walter, in surprise.

"Yes, by pilgrims and devotees."

"What simpletons, to kiss a bronze toe!"

"Mr. Tenant," said Minnie.

"What, my child?"

"Hold me up."

"What for?"

"I want to kiss that toe."

"Nonsense!" exclaimed Walter.

"When you are with the Romans, do as Romans do!" answered the child.

Mr. Tenant lifted her up, and she kissed the toe; and when she had performed the act, Walter, with a laugh, inquired if she felt any better.

"I don't get," said Walter to his father, "**an idea of the vastness of this building.**"

"No, you do not, because the whole edifice is so well proportioned that you do not perceive the vast size."

"Is that it?"

"Yes; you notice those marble figures near the door?"

"Yes, sir."

"Well, they are several times larger than life, and yet they look like babes."

"But the dome does not look so high."

"No, there is great deception there also."

"The Cathedral does not appear much larger than some churches I have seen at home."

"Yet you could put a dozen churches like the Old South in here, and have room then for thousands of people. And if you should put Park Street Spire upon the top of Bunker Hill Monument, it would but reach the dome in the centre."

"Wonderful!"

"Truly so."

When they had walked about for some time, they went up into the dome. A broad, paved, spiral staircase leads up so gradually, that most of the distance could be accomplished on the back of a donkey. The summit is obtained at the expense of weary limbs. Travellers reach the galleries within the dome, and look down upon the priests and worshippers below, who all seem like children. Still higher, it becomes difficult to distinguish them as human beings. From the outer gallery, beneath the cross, a noble view is gained of Rome, the old ruins of the past, and the broad Campagna stretching away in the clear distance. Looking down in front of the church appear the piazza, the fountains, and the obelisk; on the left stand the Vatican and the pope's palace; on the right, the famous Inquisition house; before you rises old St. Angelo; along flows the Tiber, on its banks churches, temples, and ruins.

"Will you ride up, Walter?" asked his father, who was seating Minnie on the back of a donkey.

"No, sir, I want to walk."

It was curious to see Minnie carried up in that way; but her father thought it better that she should be thus assisted.

"Minnie, your donkey looks like Don Quixote's nag before his battle with the windmill."

"You had better not say any thing, brother. You may look like Don Quixote himself *after* the battle with the windmill, before you get down."

At length they reached the summit, and went out upon the outer gallery, where they remained some time looking off upon the numerous objects in view. As they stood there Minnie exclaimed, —

"What are those?"

"Those what?" asked her father.

"Those houses on the roof beneath us," she said, pointing to some cottages on the building.

"They are houses for the workmen, who live up here."

"Live on the roof?"

"Yes; they are employed here all the time, and in those houses live their families, and it is said they seldom go down."

"I should like to live up here."

"Perhaps they will take you to board," said Walter, laughing at her.

"You would soon tire of being up here, my daughter," replied her father. "You would soon want your flower garden, and you would miss the sails you used to have in Mr. Tenant's yacht."

"I didn't think of that."

"You are a silly little girl, Min," added Walter.

"I ain't; but when I am up on such a place as this, I feel as if I always wanted to stay."

"Will you go to de ball, gentlemen?" asked the *valet de place*, very respectfully.

"Just as the rest say," answered Mr. Tenant.

"I do not care about it," said Mr. Percy. "I was put into the ball on the cathedral in London, and am not very particular for another experiment of the kind."

"O, do go, father," coaxingly pleaded Walter.

"You must, you must!" shouted Minnie.

"What do you want to go in there for, Min?" asked Mr. Tenant.

"O, just to say we have been in."

"Why not jump off here, just to say you have done it?"

"That would be unreasonable."

"Is not the other?"

"No, I think not. But I want to go to see the inside."

"Well, friend Percy, this boy and girl say so, and I suppose we must go in."

"Pe the gentlemens ready?" asked the guide.

"Yes."

Up they went into the ball, which they found would hold twelve or fifteen persons; and there they sat and conversed for a few minutes, but finding the heat very oppressive, they were soon glad to get down again.

During their stay in Rome, they often went to the Cathedral, and two or three times ascended to the gallery, but never after went into the ball, the one visit having satisfied the children. Once or twice they saw the Cathedral decorated for public festive occasions. One day, as they were retiring from the church, the conversation turned on the rites and services of the Romish church, and Mr. Tenant remarked that there was one thing they had not seen yet.

"What is that?" asked both children at once.

"The *Scala Santa*."

"What is that?" asked they.

"The Holy Staircase."

"We know no better now than before."

"The famous *Scala Santa*, or Holy Staircase, said to be the identical stairs over which Christ descended from the judgment hall of Pilate."

"Is it really the staircase?"

"Whether the identity of this relic can be proved is a question. Proof does exist to show that the house was taken down and removed to Rome, and this spacious staircase would compare very well with what we may suppose Pilate's hall to have been in other respects. Doubtless there is more proof that this is the same staircase, than there is to show the genuineness of many of the relics."

"Where is the '*Scala Santa*'?"

"Connected with St. John Lateran, a church which we have already seen."

While this conversation was going on, they had reached the place, and they found what purported to be the identical stairs which were trodden by the sacred feet of Jesus eighteen hundred years ago.

These stairs now lead to a little Gothic chapel at the top, while another parallel staircase, separated by a wall, runs up on each side. There are twenty-eight of the holy steps, and pilgrims ascend them on their knees. The number who make the ascent is so great that, a few years ago, it was found necessary to cover them with plank, lest the marble should be entirely worn away.

"Mr. Tenant," said Minnie, "won't they let any body go up, unless they go on their knees?"

"No, dear."

"But I must go up some way."

"O, no!"

"O, yes!"

"Don't let her," said Walter.

"You had better not," said her father.

"Don't act like a simpleton, Min," said Walter.

"O, do let me go up; I will go quick."

"If you wish to, my child," said her father, "you may."

"Well, I will go."

THE HOLY STAIRS.

"If you are determined to go, Minnie, I will climb with you."

"That's good, Mr. Tenant."

So they went at it on their knees. When they were half way up they paused to examine the stains said to be the blood of our Saviour, which fell from his head when he was stopped by the mob. Mr. Percy and Walter went up one of the parallel staircases, and, arriving at the top, saw Mr. Tenant and the little girl coming up upon their knees.

"Minnie, what did you see?" asked Walter.

"I saw the stain of the Saviour's blood."

"Ah, I guess you did."

"That is what they say."

"*They* say a great many things that are only impositions."

Mr. Percy turned to his friend Tenant, who stood by, silently wiping the perspiration from his forehead, and brushing his knees, as if anxious to shake the holy dust from his garments, and said to him, "Did you get paid for your pilgrimage?"

"If the church of Rome be true, I did, for she grants to any one who will climb these stairs on his knees an indulgence of forty days."

A monk, perceiving that our travellers were well-dressed persons, and probably suspecting that they were able to pay for what they saw, offered to conduct them to some relics; and they consenting, he took them to a room where they were shown the table on which it is said the "Last Supper" was celebrated, the mouth of the well at which Jesus sat with the woman of Samaria, the column of the temple which was split asunder when the veil was rent, the marble slab on which the soldiers cast lots for the garments of Christ, and various other objects of superstitious interest and regard.

"Have you seen many of these since you have been in Rome?" asked Minnie.

"Yes, several."

"What was one, pa?"

"The cradle in which Christ was rocked by the virgin Mary."

"Another."

"A stone on which are the impressions of two human feet, said to be those of Christ, the stone being one on which he stood when he said to Peter, "Thou art Peter, and on this rock I will build my church."

"What else?"

"The Santissimo Bambino."

"Pray, what is that?"

"The Holy Baby!"

"And what is the Holy Baby?"

"It is a wooden figure of the infant Saviour, carved by a monk, who, having finished it, lay down to sleep. While dreaming of paradise, St. Luke came and painted his little image, which was made out of the wood of a tree found growing on the Mount of Olives. Henceforth the figure became possessed of miraculous powers to heal diseases."

"Any more?"

"Yes, the napkin with which it is said the women who followed Christ to the cross wiped the bloody sweat from his brow."

"Have you seen what purported to be pieces of the true cross?"

"Yes, several pieces."

"Are these shown to the people?"

"Not generally."

"Then how do you get at them?"

Mr. Percy took out a five franc piece, and held it up, and smilingly remarked,—

"This is the silver key that will unlock almost any door, or open almost any gate."

During the winter the children saw many of these relics, and looked upon them with interest, but without any superstitious veneration, as they had no faith in their genuineness.

Chapter XI.

WALKS AROUND THE FORUM.

THERE is a living Rome and a dead Rome, a city of the Present, and a city of the Past. The city of the Past is in ruins; the silence of death hovers where once walked imperial conquerors, and the loathsome lizard creeps where once senators and tribunes revelled in luxury. The city of the Present is full of monks, cardinals, and priests; its public ornaments are churches, and its populace bow and rise at the sound of the sacerdotal trumpet. To the city of the Past we now bend our steps.

"And is this the Forum, of which I have heard so much?" said Walter, as one day the party stood on that spot which was once the resort of orators and statesmen.

"This is all that remains of it," replied his father.

"Was it not a noted place in ancient times?"

"Yes, my son; it was to the old Romans what Faneuil Hall was to the people of the early American states."

"What?"

"Why, the Cradle of Revolution."

"It must have been a beautiful spot originally."

"O, yes; the broken fragments which you see around you attest that."

"I should like to have heard the orators who once here stirred the hearts of the people."

"They are all gone, and the race of Romans that dwell in the city is a very different race from that which was here two thousand years ago."

Mr. Percy then led his children through the Forum, and described to them what they saw, answered their questions, pointed out arches and pillars, and interested them greatly in the place so sacred to eloquence and patriotism. True, Minnie was a little impatient, and wanted to be gone; but Walter lingered, and it was only a promise of visits to other ruins that could induce him to leave. The Coliseum came in for a visit of a day, and that gave more satisfaction than the Forum. The young reader knows that this is an immense amphitheatre, built about the time of Christ for gladiatorial purposes; and though in ruins, it still stands in its gigantic proportions, the wonder of the world.

"Here is the entrance," said Mr. Percy, as they went in.

"I remember a prophecy made by somebody," said Minnie.

"What was it?" asked Mr. Tenant, who had hold of Minnie's hand.

> "'While Rome stands the Coliseum shall stand;
> And when the world falls ——'

I can't remember the rest."

"No, I shouldn't think you could," said Walter; "you havn't got any of it right."

"Then you had better try yourself."

"I know what it is."

"Then repeat it, Walter," said Mr. Tenant.

"I can, for I have read it a hundred times. Every traveller that goes to the Coliseum repeats it; so a book I was reading yesterday said."

"Well, if you can quote it, do so, bub."

"I will if you will be quiet:

> 'While stands the Coliseum, Rome shall stand;
> When falls the Coliseum, Rome shall fall;
> And when Rome falls, the world.'"

"Bravo!" cried Minnie, clapping her hands.

They were now in the centre, and Mr. Percy called the attention of the children to the fact that on the very spot where they then stood the blood of martyrs had been shed.

THE ROMAN FORUM.

"Do you remember any one in particular, pa?" asked the little girl.

"Yes, my daughter, I remember the name of one good and great man who was here torn to pieces by wild beasts."

"Who was he?"

"He was the gentle, pious bishop of Antioch."

"And his name?"

"Was Ignatius!"

"Tell us about him."

"For heresy, he was condemned to be destroyed here."

"What kind of beasts was he thrown to?"

"Lions."

"Was he not afraid?"

"No, he did not fear death. When they put him in here, he stood a moment, as if in silent prayer, and then advanced towards the lions, who, being very hungry, sprang upon him."

"Did they tear him all to pieces?"

"They killed him, tore his flesh and drank his blood. After he was dead, two of his deacons, who had followed him with tears from Antioch to Rome, gathered up his bones, carried them away, and laid them down at the feet of the saints in Antioch."

"And what is this cross?" asked Minnie, as

she pointed to a wooden crucifix set up in the centre of the arena.

"That was put there by the priests of Rome."

"There is an inscription on it," remarked Walter.

"Go and read it Walter, and tell us what it is," said his sister.

Walter went to it, and returned, saying, "I cannot read it."

"Why not?" said Minnie.

"Because it is written in Italian, and I do not know any thing about the language."

"Mr. Tenant, will you read it?"

"If I can."

That gentleman went to the cross, and, after looking some time, told the party that as near as he could make out, not knowing much of the Italian language himself, the inscription stated, that whoever would kiss that cross was entitled to an indulgence of two hundred days.

"Then I am in for kissing it."

"You?" said Walter.

"Yes."

"What for?"

"I want the indulgence."

"Ah, you are indulged so much now that you will be a spoiled child before we return to Cambridge, unless we look out."

"Well, I mean to kiss it. I went up the *Scala Santa* on my knees, and kissed the toe in St. Peter's, and I want to kiss this. We are among Romans, you know."

So Minnie kissed the cross. Then they all went up upon the broken walls, and saw the Coliseum in the blaze of daylight. They also returned one moonlight night, and obtained a view of the edifice, when the pale rays were stealing through the broken arches — a view which Byron so much admired, and over which poets of greater claim have become rapturous.

"I should think," said Walter, as they took their seats in the carriage to return from the Coliseum, "that the old Romans must have been fond of such exhibitions, to demand a structure so large as this."

"They were very fond of gladiatorial shows and theatrical plays. This is not the only structure of the kind that you will see."

"Are there others?"

"Yes, several, of different sizes, and built in different ages."

"What are they?"

"One is the Circus Maximus, which lies in a hollow between two of the hills on which ancient Rome was built, and in its day must have been of extraordinary beauty and elegance, twenty-one hundred and eighty-seven feet long, nine hundred and sixty feet broad, and capable of seating two hundred thousand persons. It was used for chariot races, and the various other performances of the Circus."

"Magnificent!"

"It certainly was. And another was the Circus Maxentius, which is more perfect than the other, and where still remain the entrances, the apartments for the chariots, the seats for the nobility, and even the balcony of the emperor."

"Here, father — the driver is stopping at an old heap of ruins. What do we find here?"

"We shall see."

They entered a yard, passed through a garden full of fig trees, and came to some mounds of earth, stone, and mortar, overgrown with weeds.

"What was this — a tomb or a dungeon?" asked Minnie, as they brushed aside a vine, and went in.

"Neither," answered her father.

"Then it must have been the cave of some beast."

"No."

"The resort of some of the old bandits."

"No."

"What then?"

"Nothing less than the Golden House of Nero."

"What, this damp, wet mound?"

"Yes."

"I always supposed the Golden House of Nero was an elegant affair, covered with gold."

"It was once. But now it has been despoiled of its beauty; the gold and precious stones have been carried away, the works of art have been destroyed, and all that remains of it is this mound of earth."

"What a pity!"

"If you will look, Minnie," added Mr. Tenant, "you can see some traces of former beauty. Look at this arched ceiling above our heads, and see that wall which once was beautiful panel work."

"Yes, I see. Mr. Tenant, was not Nero a very bad man?"

"Yes; he was cruel, extravagant, and ambitious."

"The first a crime, the second a fault, the third a virtue," said Walter.

"Ah, Walter, you go in for ambition, do you?"

"A laudable ambition, sir. You know about the

'Youth who through an Alpine village passed,
Bearing a banner with a strange device, crying —'"

"O, fudge! Mr. Tenant, do stop Walter's poetry, and tell me about Nero."

"Well, coz, in these halls, now lonely and deserted, the monster lived and revelled in his iniquity; and the very walls seem to cry out against his crimes. His name is associated with all that is brutal and depraved in man."

"Yes, that I have always heard; but what did he do that was so wicked?"

"At the early age of seventeen he murdered one of his dearest friends in a violent fit of passion."

"What was his name?"

"Britannicus. Then, to accomplish his ambitious schemes, he murdered Agrippina."

"Who was he?"

"Not a man, but a woman, and she his mother."

"His mother?"

"Yes, to get rid of her influence, and to reign alone."

"What a wretch!"

"Then he had two tutors, Seneca and Lucan, whom he murdered in a spirit of hatred and revenge, because they remonstrated against his crimes."

"Was he married?"

"Yes; should you not like to have been his bride? You have often wished you were a queen."

"O, no, indeed — the bloody monster!"

"But his wife was an empress."

"How did he treat his wife?"

"He had more than one. One was a very unfortunate woman."

"What was her name?"

"Octavia. For things in which she was entirely guiltless, she was divorced and shut up on the Island of Pandaleria, where he visited her, and compelled her to open her veins and let out her blood."

"What a wretch!"

"He had another, Poppæa Sabina, who did not fear him at all, but rebuked his sins; and so constant were her denunciations of his crimes that he killed her to silence her voice."

"Worse and worse — what else?"

"Why, you know that on one occasion he employed men to set fire to Rome, and when it was burning went upon the roof of this Golden House and played on his viol."

"What did he want Rome to burn for?"

"He hated Christians, and when the city was set on fire, he charged it on them, and made the charge an occasion for a general massacre."

"Infamous!"

"That word does not express the enormity of his conduct."

"How did he die?"

"Committed suicide to save himself from the indignation of his people, who rose up against his crimes."

When they left the Golden House, which is not golden now, they went to the old Palace of the Cæsars, on the Palatine; and spent weeks following in visiting temples, arches, and ruined palaces. Walter was surprised at the extent of these ruins. The baths especially furnish an idea of the immense wealth and prodigality of the old Roman monarchs. Those of Caracalla cover an area of a mile in circuit, and the ruins which remain are still grand and beautiful. The fine mosaic floors, on which are piled the fallen pillars — the exquisite carvings, broken pieces of which are scattered about — speak volumes as to the former glory of the place. The baths of Diocletian, of Agrippa, of Constantine, of Titus, are but little inferior to those of Caracalla.

"There is one place I want to go to, father," said Walter, one day.

"Where?"

"To the prison where Paul was incarcerated."

"The Mamertine?"

"Yes, sir."

"We will go there to-day."

The party directed their steps to the prisons,

two in number. They are beneath the surface of the earth, directly under the Church of St. Giuseppe, and consist of two large chambers, one directly under the other. A flight of some thirty steps leads to the first chamber, which is about thirty feet square. The chamber below is somewhat smaller. Into this lower room the prisoners were formerly lowered through a hole in the ceiling, and allowed to perish most miserably. The light of the sun never penetrates that dark abode; the walls drop filth, and the floor is thick with a black, dirty mud.

As the party went down, the *valet de place* pointed to an indentation in the wall, in the form of a human head.

"What is it?" asked Mr. Tenant.

"It is the form of the head of Peter, who was once confined here," said the *valet*. "When the apostle went down, the jailer gave him a push. His head struck the wall, and made this indentation."

"Hum!" said Minnie.

"Whew!" was the response of Walter.

In the middle of the lower chamber is a pillar, to which the apostle Paul is said to have been chained; and also a fountain of cold, delicious water, which is said to have been produced by miracle.

"How was it?" asked Walter of the *valet*.

"It was this. When Peter was here, (the Romans are fond of ascribing miracles to Peter,) his jailers, Martinian and Processus, were converted to Christ, and wanted to be baptized, and to procure water for the service the apostle prayed that God would furnish it. When he arose, a fountain sweet and pure gushed up from the very spot which had been pressed by his knees."

The children tasted the water, and said that it was very cold and pleasant to the taste.

"Look there!" said the *valet*.

"What now?" inquired Mr. Tenant.

"That door leads into the Catacombs," and he opened it, and out came a dank smell, which was very unpleasant. There also rushed out a cold wind, that almost extinguished their torches.

Minnie wanted to go in a little distance, and her father consented, and she entered in the dark, while Walter stood with a torch at the door. The little girl boldly and bravely went on about one hundred feet, sometimes striking her head against the rock; but she found that the torch behind her gave her no assistance, and a lizard leaping against her arm caused her to turn back, and get out as quickly as she could.

These Catacombs wind under the city in all

directions. They were the retreat of Christians in the dreadful persecutions that occurred in the days of Nero, and are now filled with their bones. From another point our party, one day, went down into them with guides and torches.

"There is one place you have not yet taken us to, father," said Minnie, as they were riding out one day.

"I have taken you almost every where — where is the one place?"

"The Traitor's Leap."

"Ah, the Tarpeian Rock."

"Yes, sir."

"Well, we are near there now."

So they drove to the Traitor's Leap, a high, rough, abrupt precipice, on the southern side of the Capitoline Hill, some seventy or eighty feet in height.

"What gives this rock its name — Tarpeian?" asked Walter.

"It derives its name," replied his father, "from Tarpeia, the daughter of a Roman magistrate."

"Why did they give it her name?"

"Because she betrayed Rome, and, for gold, opened the gates of the city to the Sabines."

"How much did she get?"

"None. The Sabines entered, and, instead

of redeeming their pledges, they cast their shields upon her in derision, until she died beneath the weight. She was buried near the place, and the rock took her name."

" But why call it the ' Traitor's Leap ' ? "

" Because condemned criminals were brought here, and cast down upon the rocks below; this custom has expired."

What is related in this chapter, is not half of what the children saw in their " walks around the Forum," as Walter called their researches among the ruins. They went to the tomb of the Scipios, and the tomb of Caius Cestius, to the Temple of Bacchus, and the Grotto of Egeria, and to many other places, about which we doubt not children have read. Spending so long time in Rome, they did nothing huriedly, but without weariness saw all they wished to of the old and the new.

Chapter XII.

The Vatican, Inside and Out.

"Do you remember the palace of that rich banker we went into the other day, Walter?" asked his sister.

"Yes."

"Wasn't it fine?"

"Very elegant — what of it?"

"I thought it was much finer than some of the palaces of kings that we have seen."

"It was."

"What is the finest palace in the world?"

"Elegant, do you mean?"

"Yes."

"I do not know; but the Vatican, the pope's palace, that we are going to see to-day, is the most wonderful."

"What makes it so?"

"Its location, contents, and inhabitants."

"Is it larger than Buckingham?"

"Very much larger."

"Does the pope live there?"

"He does."

"Is it far off?"

"Not very far. It stands in a fine position on the left of St. Peter's, and communicates with the Castle of St. Angelo by a covered gallery. It has, Mr. Tenant tells me, eight grand staircases; two hundred of less size and elegance; twenty courts, and four thousand four hundred and twenty-two fine apartments. These apartments are filled with every thing valuable in the fine arts, and every thing beautiful in works of taste. Then the galleries extend for miles, the building itself being one thousand one hundred and fifty-one feet long, and seven hundred and sixty-seven feet wide. Here dead marble speaks with a living voice, and silent painting and lifeless canvas teach eloquent lessons."

"Quite eloquent you are, bub."

"Now don't, you plague."

"Don't what?"

"Why, don't trouble me when I am trying to enlighten you."

"Come, children," called Mr. Percy, "we are all ready to go to the Vatican."

"So are we, pa," answered Minnie.

And off they went, until they reached the palace of the pontiffs, where they alighted.

"What are those?" asked Minnie of Walter, pointing to the pope's sentinels standing in the entrance way.

"They are," replied Walter, "the Swiss guard."

"What a queer uniform they wear!"

And queer the uniform is, consisting of steel helmets, with flowing plumes; frocks of blue, green, white, and yellow stripes; loose, flowing Bloomer trousers, similarly striped; stockings striped likewise. They look quite fantastic. The party passed by the guards into the halls and galleries of the Vatican. It would take a long time to tell what they saw; but Walter noted down many things, and afterwards wrote out a full description in his journal. Among the paintings noticed by him was the great masterpiece of Raphael, the Transfiguration, which has formed an object of admiration from the day of its execution, and which, after his decease, was hung over his corpse, and worshipped by bowing, superstitious throngs; the Conversion of St. Jerome, by Domenichino, like a living scene looking down from the wall; the Crucifixion of St. Peter, by Guido, so true to nature and so just to art that tears of sympathy steal unbidden down the check; and many others.

Then they went into the galleries of sculpture, where they saw the famous Laocoön, and the sleeping Cleopatra, and many a form in marble that seems to speak to the stranger as he approaches. Then the wonderful library, with its books and manuscripts, and the sacred places which are visited by all who enter Rome, were seen.

"I want to see the Sistine Chapel," said Walter, as they wandered about.

"What is that?" asked his sister.

"The famous chapel where the pope worships."

"O, dear! I thought it was some old ruin, by the interest you manifested."

"No."

"We will go to it now, children, if you wish to," said their father.

"What is this dreary place famous for?" asked Minnie, as they entered the celebrated chapel.

"As the place where the pope performs service, or himself attends service."

"Pho!"

"There is the chair in which he sits."

"I will go and sit down in it."

"Stop, stop," cried Mr. Percy; "you may get into trouble."

The official who seemed to have the care of the chapel told Minnie she might sit in the chair, which she did, exclaiming, —

"Now I sit in the pope's chair of state."

While this was taking place, Mr. Tenant and Walter were looking at the great picture of the Last Judgment, painted by Michael Angelo, which is much defaced by time and the smoke of candles. It is sixty feet long and thirty broad. The dead are seen rising from their graves — the good and bad; the angels winging their way from the heights above and sweeping to the depths beneath, the anguish of some and the joy of others, all stand out with striking effect.

As they left the chapel, Walter expressed the desire to see the occupant of the private apartments — the pope himself; but his father told him that could not be. But as they retired from the building they saw a stir among the people; and soon the pontiff came down the grand staircase, entered his carriage, and rode away. They had a good view of him, and his countenance was at once daguerreotyped on the memories of the children.

"How is a pope raised to office?" asked Walter, as they rode home.

"When a pope dies," Mr. Percy replied, "the cardinals shut themselves up and ballot for a successor; and when the election is made, the ballots are all put into a grate, and the smoke announces to the people of Rome that a choice has been effected. Then a herald goes forth and announces who the fortunate man is."

"Do they often ballot many times?"

"Yes. When Gregory XVI. died, the cardinals, according to the usual custom, shut themselves up, and proceeded to the election of his successor. Five days were spent in an ineffectual attempt to elect some one to lead the hosts of Rome; but on the sixth it was announced that Cardinal Feretti was pope."

"Was that the pope's name?"

"Yes."

"Was that all?"

"No, his whole name is Giovanni Maria Mastai Feretti."

"Whew! enough of it."

"Is he a good man?"

"Better than many of the popes."

"Has his administration been an easy one?"

"No. In November, 1848, his people rose up against him, and he fled from Rome in the jacket of a Bavarian slave, and found shelter from his unloving subjects in the arms of Ferdinand of Naples, at Gaeta."

"Who is Ferdinand?"

"The king of Naples, you know, who has earned the title of King Bomba."

"O, yes, I should have remembered."

"How did the pope get back?" asked Minnie.

"The French came and subdued the Romans, and the pope has been sustained by French and Austrian armies ever since."

"Was the pope a cardinal once?"

"Yes; he was elected to that office in 1840. Previous to that he was an archbishop, made so in 1829."

"Is there not much lamentation in Rome when a pope dies?"

"No, not much. When Gregory XVI. died, the people seemed to be glad. And if Pius IX. should die, there would not be much mourning, if we may judge from the fact that he is now sustained on the episcopal throne by French arms."

"Do you remember when Gregory died?"

"Yes; I read the account in English and American newspapers. I recollect that it was stated, that as soon as his death was known, one of the cardinals, Camerlinque, repaired to the palace, and went through the usual formality of striking three blows on the forehead of the dead man, and announcing officially to the people of Rome that 'papa was surely dead.'"

"Did he die in the Vatican?"

"No; he breathed his last at the Quirinal Palace, which you remember to have visited a few days ago."

"What was that pope's name?"

"Mauri Capellari."

"Shall we have any opportunity to see the present pope again?"

"I think we shall."

That opportunity soon occurred. One day, soon after this conversation, the gentlemen were informed that some religious services were to be held which would give the party a fine opportunity of seeing the pope. So, getting ready as soon as possible, they hurried out. The streets were thronged with gay and animated crowds of people. French soldiers, in shining uniforms, were moving up and down the Corso; monks and nuns, friars and priests, wending their way towards the venerable and sacred edifice, St. Peter's. They soon learned that a religious procession was to be formed, and that thousands of monks and priests would go through the streets chanting their sacred lays. This news pleased the children very much. So, falling in with the line of carriages, they crossed the bridge, by St. Angelo, and soon found themselves in front of the Cathedral. They were fortunate enough to secure good seats under the colonnade, through which the procession was to pass. At nine o'clock precisely the stir began, the first rank emerging from the door of the Vatican just as the hour arrived.

"What are these grim soldiers?" asked Minnie, as a regiment of soldiers, with stern countenances and looks as grave as if they were marching to the field of death, came slowly by.

"They are French soldiers. You should know the uniform by this time," answered Walter.

"I do know it, but could not tell why French soldiers should be in this procession. Who are those now coming?"

"This is a company of the famous *gens d'armes*."

"Savage looking — are they not?"

"Yes, and ugly looking."

"Here are some boys — who are they?"

"Boys that are being educated in Catholic schools," replied the lad, as several hundred boys, wearing white robes, and carrying burning candles, and, as they moved on, sending out strains of music from their young lips, deliciously wild and discordant, went marching by.

Next followed the friars, white, gray, and black, of all the different orders, with large wax candles burning in their hands.

"How do you like the looks of them, Minnie?" asked Mr. Tenant.

"I don't like the looks of them at all."

"Why not? Some of them are good looking men."

"I should think they were. They are barefoot, unshaven, filthy, and superstitious."

The friars, priests, cardinals, having passed by, a mitre on a velvet cushion was borne by, at which the people bowed low, and then followed more monks, and all the time bells were ringing, cannon firing, and the people shouting with joy. An hour was thus occupied, when the bell of the Cathedral announced that the pope was leaving the Vatican. He came on, preceded by his body guard of soldiers, dressed in their singular uniform, which gave them a most grotesque appearance.

"What is coming?" asked Minnie.

"The pope," replied her father.

"What, mounted on men's shoulders!"

"Yes — silence!"

"O, dear," said the little girl to herself, "I can't talk; so I must look with all my eyes. Then that is the pope. Walter, Walter!" she whispered.

"What?"

"He looks as if he was seasick."

"Hush!"

The pope passed by. He rode in a car trimmed

with gold and decorated with spangles. Over his head was a canopy of gilt and crimson. The car was borne upon the shoulders of ecclesiastics and princes of high rank, and his head was bowed over a golden crucifix.

"What does he look like, Minnie?" asked Mr. Tenant.

"Like a man riding on an elephant," answered the child.

"How do you like his looks?"

"Very well. He seems mild and inoffensive. How old is he?"

"He was born in 1792. You can calculate from that."

"Let me see. From 1792 to 1800 is eight years; from 1800 to 1858 is fifty-eight years; fifty-eight and eight are sixty-six. He must be sixty-six years old."

The whole procession having passed, the party hurried to the Cathedral, where the pope performed some religious service, and gave his benediction to the populace. After this they saw His Holiness, as the pope is styled, on several occasions. The children thus became very familiar with the Vatican and its princely occupant.

Chapter XIII.

THE CARNIVAL.

"THE CARNIVAL! What is the Carnival? Every body is talking about the Carnival. People tell us not to leave Rome until Carnival is over. They ask us if we are getting ready for Carnival. Do tell me what it is?" said Minnie, hurriedly, and almost out of breath, as she had been listening one morning to the two gentlemen as they conversed about the approaching festivities.

"Minnie, are you crazy?" asked her father, disturbed by her vehemence.

"No, pa; but it seems to me that the people here are all going crazy about the carnival, and I wish to know something about it."

"Well, here is Walter; he will tell you, while I attend to some business matters with Mr. Tenant."

"Well, Walter, what about the carnival?"

"I don't know much about it; only that it is a season of festivity, continuing several weeks, when the people of Rome give themselves up to pleasure."

" How do they get it ? "

" They begin with religious services, and end with all kinds of jolly nonsense. We shall see when it comes."

They did see. The religious services which precede, rather than form a part of the carnival, soon commenced. To those who are not interested in the imposing ceremonies and gorgeous shows of the Papal church, these days drag heavily. Pleasure in the usual forms is prohibited, and the churches are filled. The religious services over, the people give themselves up to unrestrained mirth, fun without wit, frolic without sense.

" To-day," said Mr. Tenant, as they were going out one morning, " the fun commences."

" O, I am so glad!" replied Minnie.

" Why ? "

" Because Rome is so tedious during religi festivities."

" You will find nothing dull here for the next eight days."

About noon, the party, seated in an open barouche, with two gentle horses and a careful driver, that Mr. Percy had taken great pains to secure, started out to see what was going on.

They found the streets full of people, the windows all up, the houses gayly decorated, and feverish expectations reigning every where.

"What—is—that?" exclaimed the children, in one breath, as turning a corner of a street brought them in view of a horrid-looking being mounted on a gaunt, hungry-looking white horse.

"That," replied her father, "is a man rigged up to represent Death on the Pale Horse, though a funny-looking Death he is."

"Is that the way they do here in carnival?"

"Yes; one part of the sport of the few days to come consists of a succession of masquerades, races, balls, and frolics, and some of these are gay, magnificent, and foolish beyond description."

"Shall we see many more like this?"

"O, yes, hundreds of them, in all sorts of grotesque costumes, and representing all sorts of characters, human, angelic, and devilish."

They had now reached the Corso. The Corso is the broad way, the great thoroughfare of Rome; and it is here that, during carnival, pleasure appears in its most attractive forms. Families lay aside their aristocratic pride, and ride out in their carriages; strangers hire less imposing vehicles; poorer classes on foot crowd the streets, while the windows, verandas, porticoes, and balconies are filled with the delighted spectators. The route of the procession is designated, and no tide rolls in an opposite direction. Especially in the Corso is the greatest care used to prevent tumult and accident.

"How brilliant!" exclaimed Minnie, as she looked upon the crowds of people, the hangings from the windows, the gaudy colors — white, olive, red — all delightfully blended.

"We are right in the midst of it," was Walter's exclamation, as in a moment they were in the crowd, and their carriage was surrounded by the masked characters, many of whom seemed to have tortured imagination for extravagant designs.

"Father! father! see those two monkeys," cried Minnie.

"Where?"

"On the balcony of that house yonder."

"O, yes, they are men."

"What have they in their hands?"

"A cocoa-nut, as near as I can see."

"Min, Min, there is a bear walking over there."

"How natural!"

"Yes; if a Rocky Mountain grizzly should see him, he would give him a hug, thinking he had found his mate."

"Ha, ha, ha!"

"And what are these coming?" asked Mr. Tenant.

For a time they could not tell, but soon found they were ladies costumed to represent angels. The carriage in which they rode was formed to represent a hemisphere, and the idea was well carried out.

"Beautiful!" cried Minnie, clapping her hands.

"That is good," replied Walter.

Then there marched by a company of tall Roman knights of the olden time, representing a race now dead; and the crowd gave way before them, as they clanked their armor, and strode on. Then came carriage loads of young ladies dressed to represent the courts of various countries. There in one carriage were Victoria and the ladies of her court; in another, Eugenie and the ladies of her train; in another, the Empress of Austria and her ladies; in another, the Empress of Russia, with her fur-clad court, making a company which drew all eyes.

"America not represented!" cried Minnie.

"No," answered Mr. Tenant.

"O, I wish I could represent my country!" exclaimed the little girl.

"You can."

"But I have no costume."

"I put into the carriage," said her father, "a small American flag. You can have that."

"Change seats with me, Walter," shouted the child to her brother, who sat on the box with the driver.

Walter complied, and her father assisted Minnie to climb into the box with the driver. The flag was affixed to Mr. Tenant's cane, and the girl, with her curls floating upon her shoulders, her whole countenance beaming with beauty, held it aloft.

"Fall into the procession, driver," she said to that person, and he turned the carriage into the line just as the last of the carriages representing the Ottoman court went by. But that little flag was recognized and greeted with shouts. Now, a party of Americans, far from home, caught sight of it, and rent the air with "hurras," such only as Americans can give. Then a party of English, understanding the impromptu effort of the child to represent her countrywomen, joined their shouts, and made the Corso ring. Even the French and Italians applauded as they saw the stars and stripes, and soon Minnie found herself a heroine indeed. A few hours spent thus sufficed for one day, and the conveyance broke from the crowd, and was driven rapidly to the hotel. And thus day followed day, each one the exhibition becoming more grotesque.

The last two days bring out all the people of Rome, and thousands of strangers, who resort to the city for the purpose of seeing the famous sports. These days are spent in a gay frolic between men, women, and children, in which they pelt each other with flowers, sugar plums, and other confectionery, until the Corso becomes a vast trough of roses and sugar, in which the people wallow, to their great delight. The carriages are filled with men and women, young and old, gay and grave, who are armed with baskets of flowers and piles of confectionery, which they throw at others whom they may meet in the street, in other carriages, on the sidewalks, and at the windows. The actors in this scene are generally masked, and grotesquely dressed, and present a singular appearance.

To please the children, Mr. Percy procured masks for them, and a large quantity of confectionery, and wild was their delight. They rode through the streets pelting every carriage they met, and in return were all covered over with flowers and dust.

And when night came a new scene was presented. Each person has a little taper, and the fun of the thing consists in his trying to keep it burning, while every other person tries to extinguish it. Walter carried a little colored torch in one hand and in the other a rod, to which was affixed a handkerchief, with which, as he rode along, he extinguished many a taper for others. Only once was his own torch extinguished, and that was when hit by an orange from the balcony of a house by which he was passing. It is quite impossible to describe the fascinating yet foolish spectacle. The Corso becomes a cloud of fire, which shines out from many a torch and lantern. Red, green, blue, and many a gay color flashes on the sight, until the whole scene becomes one of bewildering beauty.

"Father, when does the carnival close?" asked Minnie, one day.

"Do you want it to close?"

"No, indeed; but I shall grow mad with excitement and delight, if these scenes continue much longer."

"Well, to-night will be the last spectacle you will wish to witness."

"Ah! what is that?"

"What you have often heard about — the illumination of St. Peter's."

"O, yes, yes, yes!"

"When we have seen that, we shall be ready to leave Rome."

"When will it occur."

"To-night."

"Is it possible?"

"You will see."

That evening they went out to see the illumination. The children, at the suggestion of Mr. Percy, had slept a few hours in the afternoon, and at nightfall were fresh and vigorous. They rode out to the Pincian Hill, from which a fine view is obtained. This illumination is deemed a grand occasion, and draws to Rome thousands of persons. The whole Cathedral is so lighted at night as to show the proportions of the building, with each pillar and projection, so that the whole appears to be one mass of fire, blazing out, hour after hour, with great architectural precision, a palace of flame, the admiration of thousands who have travelled far to gaze upon it.

"O, look! see!" was the exclamation of Walter, and the whole company turned towards the Cathedral. The grand exhibition had commenced, and soon the whole edifice was wrapped in soft silver light.

"This is the silver illumination," said Mr. Percy.

"Why called so?" asked Walter.

"Because the light is white, as you see."

"How is it produced?"

"It is produced by the lighting of about six thousand lanterns, formed of white paper, so as to give the effect of a white light."

For a long time they gazed upon this silver illumination, and while it continued, the building seemed to be one sheet of silver, glistening in some supernatural light, and shining on, hour after hour, with a subduing aspect.

"And what now?" asked Walter, as the Cathedral seemed to blaze again, about ten o'clock.

"The golden illumination has commenced," replied his father.

"How is it done?"

"By the addition of several thousand more lights, made of tar and other inflammable materials, which are made to flash out at once, changing the whole appearance of the scene."

"How do they get the lights there?"

"Several hundred men lower themselves upon that mighty dome, and hang there amid the fire, perilling their lives for the generous compensation which they receive."

"It is wonderful!" said the thoughtful boy, who had never seen its like before.

"It is perfectly splendid," was the declaration of his more vivacious sister.

And wonderful and splendid the spectacle was, as it shone that night. In the midst of the flood of light, the Cathedral stands, one mass of fire, yet unconsumed. The bright light reveals every column, crevice, window, and door, and the church stands like a mountain of fire, surmounted by a cross which now seems lost in the clouds, and anon stands out with great distinctness. All night it burns and blazes there, while none in Rome thinks of sleep. The scene is too exciting; and, till the last light goes out in the dim gray of the morning, the Pincian Hill is covered with a dense mass of spectators.

"Back to the hotel," said Mr. Percy to the driver.

"Not yet, pa," pleaded Minnie.

"No, not yet, father," urged Walter.

"It is one o'clock, and will be two before you are in bed."

"We shall not sleep, if we retire," said Walter, "and we might as well sit up."

"I think we must return, children; you are already much excited."

The driver turned his horses towards the hotel, and the children were soon in bed — but not to sleep. The scenes they had witnessed, weary though they were, would have kept them awake even if the hotel and the streets had not been filled with crowds of noisy people. Morning dawned ere slumber descended upon their grateful eyelids. And even then, in their dreams, they lived the night over again, and in visions saw that Cathedral blaze in the air, while shouts from ten thousand tongues fell on their ears. Often they started from their sleep with exclamations of delight and wonder, and sank back upon their pillows only to enjoy the spectacle over again; and when they woke, it was with the magnificent scene pictured indelibly on the tablets of memory.

Chapter XIV.

NAPLES.

"GET up, Walter, get up," was a cry raised by Minnie, one morning, very soon after the events recorded in the foregoing chapter.

"Go away and let me alone," answered the boy.

"Get up, get up; we are entering the Bay of Naples."

"What!"

"What? sleepy head; wake up!"

"What did you say?"

"We are entering the Bay of Naples — father has been up an hour — passengers all on deck — glorious morning — time you were out of your berth," was the cheerful answer, given in one breath, by the child, as she hurried from the cabin to the deck.

The party had gone from Rome to Civita Vecchia, a very mean town on the coast, and there taken a steamer for Naples, the beautiful bay of which the steamer, the Erculano, was now entering. Walter hurried on his clothes, vexed with himself for having overslept, and was soon on deck, where he found the passengers expressing their admiration of the enchanting scene.

"Here comes bub, an hour late," was Minnie's salutation, who was glad to have found Walter a little behind herself. But he did not notice her remark. His attention was drawn to what he saw before him — the bay and city of Naples, and the surrounding country. "Beautiful!" he repeated, as he reached his father's side.

"Ah, Walter, you here? We have been trying to make out the secret of the beauty of this bay," said Mr. Percy.

"Is there any secret about it?"

"Yes; we know it is beautiful, but what the elements of that beauty are, one does not see at the first glance."

"Have you discovered the secret?"

"Yes. The beauty of the bay arises from a variety of circumstances. Its form is regularly curved, and all around are shining palaces, looking down upon its shores, and off upon its waters. Behind the towns and villages, the hills and mountains rise abruptly, and seem to stand as high towers charged with molten torrents, which they are ready to **pour out upon the surrounding country.**"

"Charming scene! I do not wonder at the old saying."

"What do you refer to?"

"'See Naples, and die.'"

"Ah, yes, that is an old saying. But we must go ashore. The steamer has come to anchor."

An hour after they were on shore, having escaped from the hungry boatmen, custom-house officials, and policemen. As they were on the way to the hotel, Walter asked, —

"How many inhabitants are there in Naples?"

"About three hundred and fifty thousand," replied his father; "but there does not appear to be so many. On approaching the city from the sea, one would hardly imagine how many human beings are huddled together. The streets are narrow; the houses, as you see, rise story on story, until they lose themselves from the view of the gazer, and both streets and houses are crowded with as miserable and dirty a class of beings as can be found in Italy."

"How much territory does the city occupy?"

"It is twelve miles in circuit, with ample fortifications; three hundred churches; forty asylums for the poor and orphans; with a vast variety of objects connected with the past and the present, to interest the traveller."

Our party spent a few weeks in Naples, and a letter from Walter to his mother will tell what they saw in that city.

NAPLES, 1859.

DEAR MOTHER: —

I wish you were here, so that I could lean my head against your shoulder, and tell you what I have seen. But as you are not here I must write to you. My letters from Rome told you all about St. Peter's, the Vatican, the Coliseum, the Carnival, and the Pope. We are now in Naples, where we have been much pleased. I know you would like to have me tell you about the people — how they look, and dress, and live. I will try to tell you, in the best language I can. The better class of the people dress very neatly, and on gala days the crowded streets present a gay and brilliant spectacle. The soldiers in uniform, with waving plumes, and the young women, with their muslin scarfs, and gay, laughing features, give a showy appearance to the whole town. But the lower order of Neapolitans are very meanly clad, and approach a step nearer barbarism than any people I have previously seen. The men wear a coarse crash shirt, with coarse trousers, which are tied around the waist with a cord. An old straw hat completes the rig. The legs and feet from the knees downward, the arms from the elbows, and the shoulders, brown and sunburnt, are generally uncovered. As to shoes, they are a luxury which the poorer people seldom indulge in. The women dress correspondingly, and are seen moving through the streets singing, with loads upon their shoulders which would almost break the back of a donkey.

Of the many things we have seen, the sheet on which I write would not suffice to tell you. We have been into monasteries and seen the monks; we have been down into the catacombs, which are in three stories or stratums, hewn out of the rock, running under the whole city, and extending as far as Pozzuoli. All along these arched subterranean passages are niches cut in the walls, just large enough for the corpse, whether it be man or child. The ceilings are adorned with mosaics and frescoes. Some of these are pagan, and some are Christian, teaching the lessons of several different ages. Little monuments with inscriptions, one to the god of gardens, are set up here, and they seem to live and speak as the red glare of the torch falls upon them. We have been to the tomb of Virgil. It stands over the entrance of the Grotto of Posilipo, in a spot to which the ashes were removed by Augustus. We pushed our way out of the city, up the hill, passing through an old gate, into a garden fragrant with flowers, and shady with fig, chestnut, and palm trees, to a little arch-like building about twenty feet long and fifteen feet wide, over which the ilex tree, so loved by Virgil, casts its shadow.

We have also visited many churches,— for you know this is a city of churches,— and they are all filled with pictures and statues. Of one of these churches let me tell you particularly. It is the cathedral, and was formerly a pagan temple; and near the door at which we entered was an urn which once contained the blood shed in sacrifices. Within is St. January's Chapel, and a very fine thing it is. It has a brass gate, which, we were told, required the labor of two men forty-five years to build it. The interior of the chapel is very richly finished; the dome small, but very superb. The altar is of gold and precious stones, and nothing but a silver bribe will uncover it. In the sacristy are kept forty-six silver busts, as large as life, of St. Antonio, John the Baptist, and others. Behind a statue of St. January is an oratory, where a golden bust of the saint, and a bottle of his blood, are kept.

And what story do you think they have about this blood? I will tell you. Father tells me that the story is this: When St. January was killed for his love to Jesus, a woman caught his blood, and preserved it. A part of the blood was taken to Spain, and the remainder to Naples. The portion brought to Naples was bottled, and, with the golden bust which contains the skull of the saint, or somebody else, is shut up in a silver tabernacle. The bust is separated from the blood; and it was told us that, when the skull and the blood are brought into contact, a miracle is produced. The coagulated blood liquefies as soon as it is brought to the bust.

I wish I had time to tell you of all the things we have seen in this strange country; but my paper is full. Besides, I hear notes of preparation for a tour we are to take to-day into the country around Naples, and Minnie is in the hall shouting my name with all her might; so I must close here.

WALTER.

"Walter, Walter, we are all waiting for you!" shouted Minnie, in the hall.

"Yes, yes, child!"

"Well, come; pa is ready, and the carriage is at the door."

Walter put his letter into his portfolio, and ran down; and soon the whole company were seated in the carriage, and on their way.

"What is this we are coming into? Mercy! how dark it is!" said Minnie.

"Yes, it is very dark," replied her father.

"What is it — a tunnel?"

"Yes, child; a wide road dug out under a mountain, called the Grotto of Posilipo."

"How long is it?"

"Half a mile, and one hundred and fifty feet high."

They passed through the grotto, and after an hour's ride came to an ancient town, in the appearance of which the children saw that the gentlemen were much interested.

"What town is it?" asked Walter.

"This is ancient Puteoli, where Paul tarried seven days, when he was on his way to Rome; and here we are at the old bridge of Caligula, now in ruins, and the pier at which Paul landed is there where those gentlemen and ladies are standing," said Mr. Percy, pointing to a group of persons near them.

They went to the pier; Walter stood where Paul is said to have stood, and then the party passed on, and at length reached a beautiful little lake.

"What lake is this?" asked Walter.

"A lake? a frog pond, more like!" responded his sister.

"This, my son, is Lake Avernus, in which Strabo says the Cimmerians, a race of fortune-tellers, lived in caves never lighted by the rays of the sun. This little ruin on the shore is the Temple of Apollo, where Æneas went to consult the Sibyls and the gods; and the forest behind is that in which he found the golden branch."

"Tell me the story, pa," said Minnie.

"We have no time now. Walter will do so when we return to the hotel."

"Will you, Walter?"

"Yes, sis. But, father, where is Sibyl's Cave?"

"Just here — don't you see those men?"

"Yes, sir."

"They are guides, who will go with us into the cave."

After some argument with the men, each one took a torch made of hemp, rosin, and tar, four feet long and two inches square, and descended through a long, dark passage, begrimed with soot and smoke, slimy and slippery, damp as death, and hissing with reptiles. This long passage leads to the Chambers and Baths of the Sibyls, which were once dry, and beautifully decorated and frescoed. They were forced to explore these chambers on the shoulders of men, the water in them being several feet deep. Several hideous, dirty, filthy-looking old fellows had followed the party some miles for the purpose of taking them in; and when they had reached the water, they mounted each the shoulders of a cicerone, and on they went. Walter sat as quietly as could be on the shoulders of his bearer; but Minnie, knowing that the man who carried her could not understand a word of English, made herself and the whole party quite merry. The descent is really amusing. The waters splash as the men pass along; the torches gleam, and cast out an unearthly light; the human horses keep up an incessant sound, half way between a snort and a groan; and the caverns below us seem to echo with the music of the Sibyls.

"Walter," shouted Minnie, "my nag is wind-broken — hear how he breathes."

"Be still, sis."

"I can't be still on this trotter."

"You will fall off."

"No, I won't; I am holding on to the fellow's mane. I say, Mr. Tenant, isn't father spoiling that new white beaver of his against the smutty wall?"

"I don't know any thing about your father's

beaver; it is as much as I can do to keep on this fellow's shoulders."

Thus they went down into the subterranean chambers, and, having rested a while, were borne out by the men, as they came in.

Passing the Baths of Nero, the Temples of Diana, Mercury, and Venus, — which are now in ruins, having few traces of their former magnificence, the beautiful vine called "Venus hair," creeping over the broken walls, and covering the spot where once stood the altar, — by the Julian Port, the Elysian Fields, and the River Styx, immortalized by Virgil, they came to Nero's celebrated prisons, which are under the spot where once stood the villa where the inhuman monster killed his mother. Here they rested, took refreshments, and prepared to return.

On their way they came to Lake Agnano, which is a pond of water in the bed of an extinct volcano; and, after riding along the shore, the *valet de place* called upon the driver to stop. He did so, and they all left the carriage.

"What now?" asked Walter.

"We are going to see the Dog Grotto."

"What is that?"

"You will see."

They reached the cave, and found it a very peculiar one. A vapor rises from the ground which is fatal to life. A torch brought into contact with it is immediately extinguished, and a dog bound and thrown upon the ground will die in two minutes. A pistol, loaded in the best manner, could not be discharged when held near the ground.

Mr. Tenant took a pistol, and loaded it in the presence of the company.

"O, what is that man going to do?" cried Minnie.

"Try an experiment, sis."

"He will kill some of us—he is terribly careless."

Mr. Tenant now went to the mouth of the cave, and holding his pistol near the ground, tried to discharge it, but could not do so. The pistol might as well have been loaded with sand. He then raised the weapon, and fired in the air. The experiment was tried by Mr. Percy and Walter, with the same result.

A man now came forward, dragging a dog. The creature howled pitifully as he was drawn roughly forward.

"Is he mad?" asked Minnie.

"No," replied Walter.

"Are they going to kill him?"

"No."

"What then?"

" Try another experiment."

" It is too bad!"

" It does seem cruel."

The man took the dog and threw him into the cave, and the poor creature sunk powerless to the ground. He was allowed to remain about eighty seconds, and then taken out, nearly dead, but was resuscitated by being thrown into cold water.

" This is singular," said Minnie to her brother.

" Yes, it is."

" What did you call the cave."

" The Dog Grotto."

" That is English."

" Yes; it is called here *Grotta del Cane*, and sometimes the ' Cavern of Charon.' "

They then went to another cave, in which ammonia gas rises from the ground. The earth is cold, and yet an intense heat arises from it; and, though no draught of wind can be perceived, one feels all the heat and gentle influence which are derived while standing over the register of a large furnace. The effect of inhaling the gas is highly exhilarating, and one would soon become intoxicated, as with opium or ether.

" I am intoxicated!" cried Minnie.

"I can't hardly stand," said Walter.

"I am not much better off," added Mr. Percy, whose head felt heavy, and who was aware of the bewildering effects of the inhalation.

But they soon recovered, went on to the sulphur baths, where one needs no fire to keep him warm. The apartments are small, rude, and covered with incrustations and saline deposits, and are formed by the sulphureous gases. Minnie wanted to be shut up in one of the apartments, and the door was closed. She remained a few minutes, when her cry for liberty was heard; and as she emerged the perspiration was pouring from her face like rain.

They all laughed at her.

"You may laugh as much as you please. I have taken a sweat in one of the fire chambers of Mount Vesuvius, and that is more than either of you can say."

They were now admonished by the driver that it was time to return to the city, as the sun was setting; and soon they were rolling along the crowded streets of Naples.

Chapter XV.

CLIMBING VESUVIUS.

"SHALL we go to-night?" asked Minnie of her brother.

"Yes."

"Why in the night?"

"Because we wish to be on the mountain at sunrise."

"It will be delightful."

"We can tell better twenty-four hours from now."

"Very true."

The reader will see that this conversation between the children relates to the ascent of Vesuvius, which was planned for that night. The children retired early, and were called at midnight, and the party at once set out. They rode in a carriage as far as Portici, where the carriage was exchanged for saddle horses. They had not gone far before Walter's horse stumbled and fell; but being a good rider, the lad was not injured, or even frightened. He, however, exchanged his stumbling horse for the one rode by the *valet de place*, and they all went on. Minnie found the ride much easier than she expected, and Mr. Tenant keeping constantly at her side, she was not afraid. They left the green vegetation far below, and went climbing up amid huge masses of lava and red rocks, into regions more and more dreary and desolate. At the Hermitage and the Observatory they rested and took refreshments, and then pressed onward. The poor beasts picked out their way amid the fallen blocks of lava, now leaping across ravines, and then rubbing their sides against the torn and ragged masses, until the bridle became useless, and the riders gave themselves up to the instincts of the animals on which they rode. About three hours after starting from Naples, they arrived at the base of the cone, and fastened their horses in the crater of an extinct volcano, or rather an old crater of the still trembling and fiery Vesuvius.

"How are we going up this steep cone?" asked Minnie.

"I don't know," replied Walter.

But the question was soon decided. Several men appeared who were accustomed to climbing, and these men each had a leather thong, one end of which was fastened to his shoulders, and the other end was given to the travellers. Minnie was seated in a sort of chair, made of rope, and carried up. Up they went. The cone is desperately steep, and they were obliged to clamber up over rough, rolling pieces of lava, which are set in motion as the foot treads upon them, and frequently three steps are taken backward where one is set forward. The men gave the party much assistance, and they reached the summit just at sunrise.

"How different from what I expected!" said Minnie, in surprise.

"Why! what difference?" asked Walter.

"Why, at a distance, Vesuvius looks like a sugar loaf, with a small, flat surface at the summit, from which a cloud of smoke is continually ascending."

"Well!"

"On reaching the apex, we find that what appears to be a level plain is a tunnel-shaped crater, with its yawning mouth about one third of a mile across, and verging to a conical point in the centre."

"How magnificent this is!"

"Yes; but the ground under our feet is hot, and little crevices are emitting steam and smoke."

"Yes, and what if the thin crust should give way and let you fall in!"

"Pho! there is no danger!"

They walked all around the crater, and cast

stones into the abyss, which, rolling down the sides, gathered great velocity as they went, and tumbled into the cavern below.

"I am hungry," said Minnie.

"I am not; I think I never should be hungry in the midst of such wonders."

"Hum! that is nonsense."

"I have arranged for breakfast," said Mr. Tenant, overhearing the conversation.

"Have you, Mr. Thoughtful? I am glad of it," added Minnie.

"How can we get breakfast here?" queried Walter.

"I have brought some eggs and other things."

"Boiled eggs?" asked Walter.

"No."

"Then how can they be cooked?"

"You don't want to cook them," interrupted Minnie; "any body as poetical as you, who, a moment ago, said you should never be hungry here, can as well eat them raw as boiled."

"We will roast them," said Mr. Tenant.

"How?"

"We will see," said the gentleman; "the eggs we will cook in one of the little veins beneath our feet."

"Can you do that?"

"We will see."

With a cane the soil was opened, and the eggs put in and covered up, and, in a few minutes, were taken out well roasted, and ready for their rocky table, and the breakfast was devoured speedily, for all had excellent appetites. After the breakfast was completed, the guides formed a kind of seat, and they all sat down to enjoy the view presented, which was very fine.

"The mountain is very quiet now — is it not, father?" said Walter.

"Yes, my son."

"When was the first eruption?"

"The first of which we have any authentic account is that which buried Herculaneum and Pompeii."

"What others?"

"In almost every century since, there have been violent eruptions."

"Any very violent ones?"

"Yes. That of 1794 shook down and overwhelmed the houses of Torre del Greco, a town of some twenty thousand inhabitants; that of 1822 sent forth such showers of ashes, that they were flying for more than a hundred miles, and the sun was darkened at noonday the region round about."

"I wish there could be one while we are here."

"There will not be."

"How do you know?"

"It takes the mountain some time to work itself up. You see it is quiet now. When an eruption takes place, warning is always given."

"Was it so when Pompeii was destroyed?"

"Yes; though not as much warning as usual, was given them."

"I have read somewhere that it came on so suddenly that Pliny the elder did not have time to escape."

"The mountain gave warning enough, but the inhabitants of Pompeii did not think their city would be reached by the deluge of fire. The elder Pliny was the victim of his own hazardous nature."

"How so?"

"The younger Pliny says of his uncle, 'The extraordinary phenomenon excited my uncle's philosophical curiosity to take a nearer view of it. He ordered a light vessel to be got ready, and gave me the liberty, if I thought proper, to attend him. I rather chose to continue my studies; for, as it happened, he had given me an employment of that kind. When, hastening to the place from whence others fled with the utmost terror, he steered his direct course to the point of danger, and with so much calmness and presence of mind, as to be able to make and dictate his observations upon the motion and figure of that dreadful scene. He was now so nigh the mountain, that the cinders, which grew thicker and hotter the nearer he approached, fell into the ships, together with pumice stones, and black pieces of burning rock. They were likewise in danger not only of being aground by the sudden retreat of the sea, but also from the vast fragments which rolled down from the mountain, and obstructed all the shore.' So you see he might have escaped if he had made the effort."

The party remained on the mountain a long time, and then prepared to descend.

" I shall tear my feet all to pieces going down over these rocks," said Walter to his father.

" You do not go down over the lava, in the way you came up."

" Ah, why not ? "

" It would be attended with danger."

" How so ? "

" Why, these pieces of lava would begin to roll, and very soon you would be rolling with them."

" I see. But how do we get down ? "

" On the other side the mountain is covered with ashes, and you go down in the soft dust."

CLIMBING VESUVIUS. 203

And soon they were on their way down, in a most amusing way. Convulsed with laughter, and shouting to each other, they descended nearly ten feet at a leap, sinking in the soft, flowing ashes as if it were light, drifting snow, raising a cloud of dust, and setting the yielding body in motion all around.

Soon they were trotting back towards Naples, and when they reached the city, they were all very tired and hungry, and were glad to seek a bath and a dinner, and afterwards a quiet talk in their own rooms.

"I wish I could converse with some one who has seen a violent eruption," said Walter, at the dinner table.

"You can," replied his father.

"How?"

"Books enable us to converse with the dead."

"But who has described the scene."

"Pliny and others."

"How did Pliny describe it?"

"His own words are, 'I cannot give a more exact description of its figure than by resembling it to that of a pine tree; for it shot up to a great height in the form of a trunk, which extended itself at the top into a sort of branches, occasioned, I imagine, either by a sudden gust of air that impelled it, the force of which decreased as it advanced upwards, or the cloud itself, being pressed back again by its own weight, expanded in this manner. It appeared sometimes bright and sometimes dark and spotted, as it was more or less impregnated with earth and cinders.'"

"There have been many very accurate and graphic descriptions of the eruptions given by scientific men, who have witnessed them," added Mr. Tenant.

"I wish I could see it with my own eyes."

"That cannot be. Imagination must supply the rest."

Thus engaged in conversation, the party sat until the evening came, and they retired to rest, with the understanding that they should sleep as long as possible in the morning, as they all had need of rest.

Chapter XVI.

THE BURIED CITIES.

"How far to Pompeii?" asked Walter, as one morning they rode out of the city of Naples, on their way to the exhumed ruins of those towns that eighteen hundred years ago were overwhelmed.

"About twelve miles, to the north-east," replied his father.

"When was the city overwhelmed?"

"It was partly shaken down by an earthquake, A. D. 63, but the enterprising inhabitants soon repaired their shattered tenements, and erected their theatres and halls of justice with more beauty and elegance than before."

"And again overwhelmed?"

"Yes. A few years rolled on, and a more general destruction occurred, and the history of Pompeii came to a sudden and terrible end."

"When was it?"

"In A. D. 79."

"Many of the people were killed—were they not?"

"Yes."

"I think you said, when we visited Vesuvius, that the mountain at that time gave warning."

"Yes, I did say so. The surrounding hills gave evidence of convulsions. The lakes and ponds in the neighborhood were affected. They rose and fell; retreated from the shores, and anon dashed up again upon the banks. Strange, unearthly sounds, like the rumbling of a thousand chariots over hollow pavements, were heard. Now and then, an opening chasm, emitting sulphureous clouds, which hung like a sable pall over the doomed city, would be seen; and at intervals a jet of flame, thrown into the air, would fall just without the walls, as if the mighty powers below were at play with the fears of men."

"Why did not the people fly?"

"They did, but soon returned to their places."

"And then, when the storm began to fall, what did they do?"

"The utmost terror seized them, and the confusion and distress were terrible."

"How much of Pompeii has been exhumed?"

"About forty acres."

"How much of Herculaneum?"

"Only a few buildings."

"Why so little?"

"Because it is much harder to make the excavations at Herculaneum than at Pompeii."

"Why so?"

"Herculaneum was buried by the lava storm, which poured along the streets, deluging the houses, consuming the verdure, and overwhelming every sign of life and beauty. Owing to the fact that this city was destroyed by lava, but few excavations have been made. The work is so slow and tedious, and requires so much labor and expense, that but little has yet been done. A large town is also built upon the spot, and the habitations of the living rise upon the tombs of the dead."

"And what was Pompeii buried with? I always thought it was lava."

"No. Pompeii was buried by a shower of ashes, and the work of exhuming it has been more speedy and successful. These ashes fell so fast that many had no opportunity to escape, or were buried in the streets as they were pursuing their way to the distant sea."

"Why were not these cities sooner exhumed?"

"It was not known where they were."

"Ah! When were they discovered?"

"The first traces of the buried cities were discovered in 1738, by Charles, King of Spain, who conquered Naples, and made Portici, a town which is built upon the ruins of Herculaneum, his residence. In sinking a well, three statues were found, which led to explorations, and resulted in the discovery of the long-buried city In 1750 Pompeii was discovered, after having remained concealed from view nearly seventeen centuries."

They had now reached Herculaneum, and with torches in their hands they went down the rocky pathway, and saw the ruins of an old theatre, and one or two other buildings; and, as there was not much to be seen they hurried on to Pompeii, and entered the city by the famous Appian Way. There they found the pavements, the houses, the columns, as they were when, eighteen centuries ago, the torrent fell upon them; the shops of the traders, with the signs still up; the frescoes on the walls, as bright and lively as ever; the mosaics of stone and shell, all clear and distinct as they ever were.

"I want you to take notice of this place, children," said Mr. Percy.

"Why so," they both asked.

"Because here a sentinel was found standing at his post of duty."

"O, yes," said Walter. "I remember Rev. Mr. K—— spoke of that in a sermon once."

"What did he say?"

"That this man was on duty, and chose death in preference to flight; and his skeleton was found in the coat of mail, with his spear in his hand."

"True; it was so."

"He must have been a faithful soldier."

"Yes; but notice this spot, marked by this large flat stone, children!"

"What of that?"

"Here were found a woman and three children. When found one of the babes was at the breast, showing that he died in the act of nursing."

Passing on they came to the house of Diomede.

"Diomede! Diomede!" Minnie repeated to herself; "it appears to me I have heard of Diomede."

"Yes, sis; Harry St. Clair was reading a story about Pompeii when we were at his house, a long time ago."

"I remember now, something was said in the story about Diomede."

"Yes, and here is his house, father says."

"Tell me about it, father!"

"You see the house is near the foot of the mountain, and was probably destroyed soon after the eruptions commenced."

"Did the occupants escape?"

"No, seventeen skeletons were found here."

"Why did they not get away?"

"They, probably supposing that the storm of fire and ashes would soon abate, retired to the subterranean passages below, with lights, and food, and wine, and there perished."

"Were they all grown-up people?"

"No, one of them was a babe. Two others were children; and when the skeletons were found some of the hair was on the skull."

"Was there any little girl, like me?"

"Yes, one; the little daughter of Diomede, the impression of whose rounded chest, made in the consolidated scoria, still is shown at Naples— the flesh consumed, but the bust remains to tell even the texture of the dress, as well as the finished beauty of the neck and arms."

"Did they find Diomede himself?"

"Yes; he was found in his garden with a bunch of keys in his hand, and near by him a slave, with some silver vases and several gold and silver coins."

"What a terrible death it must have been!"

"And here," said Mr. Percy, as they had advanced some distance into the place, "is a prison."

"What was found here?"

"Two men were found with their feet fast in

the stocks. They were condemned to sit there a few days, but an awful Providence turned the sentence into one far more terrible; and there, for seventeen centuries, they sat, ere friendly hands came to undo the stocks and let them out."

"I should like to have been here when they were taken out," said Minnie.

"Why — for what purpose?"

"To have seen with my own eyes."

"Whose eyes should you see with if not your own, coz?" asked Walter.

"Well, I cannot hardly believe that all these persons were found buried here."

"What building is this, father?" asked Walter, coming to a ruin more perfect than most they had seen.

"This is the temple of Isis."

"What, the idol?"

"Yes."

"Was it full of people?"

"No; but near the door of the temple was found a skeleton of one of the priests, drawn into the temple, perhaps for plunder, and perhaps for devotion, at the awful hour when the city was being overwhelmed; the ashes, pressing against the door without, rendered escape impossible."

"Was that the only one found?"

"No, there were others."

"Do tell us about them!"

"In one room a priest was found at the table eating."

"Eating at such an hour?" asked Minnie.

"Yes."

"How could they tell?"

"The remains of his dinner were before him. The remnant of an egg and the limb of a fowl, tell us on what he was making his repast."

"But the ashes would not have stopped his eating."

"He was probably suffocated by the noxious gas that came in."

"Was there any other?"

"Yes; a priest was found with some money in his hand, showing that he had come back at that awful hour to rob the temple."

"Any more?"

"Yes, one man more. He was found near a door, with an axe in his hand, and on the door were the marks of the blows."

The party then entered some of the shops — the barber's shop, the apothecary's store, the butcher's stall. In the baker's shops were found the ovens ready for use, the mills in which the grain was broken, the kneading troughs, the various

A STREET IN POMPEII.

articles used in the making of bread, and the bread itself, well done. In the butcher's stall meat well cooked was found.

When they had seen the shops, they sought out some of the houses of the noted citizens, and the public buildings of the city. The house of Sallust was once a magnificent structure, and the remains still bear many marks of beauty and finish; the house of Pansa is traced out, well arranged, spacious, and splendid, even in its ruins. The doorway still remains, with its beautiful Corinthian pilasters. The house of the tragic poet, so called, which was exhumed in 1824, is an object of great interest. The various apartments are full as the walls can hang with historical paintings.

As they walked about they met an old woman, withered and haggard, who looked as if she might have been the witch of the burning fields, who followed them, muttering as if she wished to express her hatred. They threw her a piece of money, and she turned back. They also saw at the House of the Fountains — so called because fountains are the most prominent things found in it — a poor, pale, blind girl, who heard them as they approached, and held out her hand.

"This is the Nydia of romance," said Mr. Tenant.

"Let us see what she wants," said Walter.

"Pictures," she said, as they drew near.

"Ah, yes; you have pictures, and you speak English."

"A little."

They found she had pictorial representations of the drawings and frescoes found on the walls of the houses, and they bought several. Walter was very particular in making his selections. He bought Jupiter wedding the unwilling Thetis to a mortal; the priests of Diana engaged in preparing for the human sacrifice; the great chariot race between the gods; the battle of the Amazons; and many others.

The frescoes are as bright and lively as the day they were put on, showing that the ancients must have had some secret in the mixing of colors which we do not now possess.

The party afterwards saw in the Museum at Naples all sorts of things taken from Pompeii, among which are the ancient stocks in which the two skeletons were found made fast; the skull of the sentinel, in his rusty armor, as he was found at the gate, on duty still in death; the petrified body of Diomede; a statue found in the Temple of Isis; an alabaster jar of fragrant balsam, nearly two thousand years old, in a tolerable state of preservation, as it was taken from an apothecary shop; chandeliers from the house of Diomede; jewelry, rings, pins, cameos, of all sizes, and of immense value, taken from the limbs of the skeletons; cooking utensils, of all kinds, from a tin pot to a cook stove; with all of which the children were much interested. They were very much pleased with the eggs, meat, soup, bread, fruit of various kinds, so wonderfully preserved that none could mistake them.

"It has been a wonderful day!" said Mr. Tenant, as the party assembled in the evening, after having visited Pompeii, in their hotel.

"It has so, indeed," replied Mr. Percy.

"I noticed," said Walter, "that the town of Portici was built up over the ruins of Herculaneum."

"Yes," replied his father.

"May not that place be destroyed?"

"Yes, it is liable to destruction every day."

"How sad it would be!"

"We hope such an event will not happen, but none can tell."

"I shall never forget this day."

"Nor shall I," added Minnie.

"Well, children, go to bed now, and, forgetting all you have seen and heard, sleep so **soundly**, that you will not even dream, and you will rise refreshed to-morrow."

"I want to dream, pa!" said Minnie.

"You do!"

"Yes, sir."

"Of what? these buried cities, skeletons, and volcanoes?"

"O, no indeed!"

"Of what then?"

"Of Home!"

Chapter XVII.

COASTWISE.

"How does the glass stand to-day?" asked Mr. Percy of Walter, who had been reaching up to a thermometer that was given him by a neighbor, Mr. Cushman, just before he sailed.

"Eighty in the shade."

"It is getting too hot for us to stay in Naples."

"Well, father, Minnie has been ready to leave for several days, and I am sure I shall be glad to move into a cooler region. My winter clothes are getting uncomfortable, and changing about as we do, I do not like to put on a thin suit."

"I learn," added Mr. Tenant, "that almost all the Americans in Naples are leaving. Mr. Daubney, whose girls Minnie frollicked so with, during carnival in Rome, took his family away last week. Mr. Seymour and family go to-morrow; and, as we have seen all we want to of Naples, I suggest that we go with them, on board the Romagna, in which they will sail for Genoa."

"But are we all ready?"

"I am."

"So am I," added Walter.

"Are you, Minnie?"

"Yes, sir."

"Are your clothes all in order, your linens all washed, and your trunk in packing order?"

"Yes, sir — can be ready in half an hour."

"O, we do not wish to hurry off so soon as that."

"Then to-morrow morning."

"If all are ready, I have no objection to going in the Romagna. I will walk down and engage passage for the company. I will get a family ticket, including four persons, for it will come cheaper."

"A family ticket?" queried Minnie.

"Yes, dear!"

"Well — but — how?"

"'Well — but — how' what?"

"I was thinking, if you had a ticket for a family, what part of the family Mr. Tenant would be."

"We can count him in."

"But you are father, we are the children. Mr. Tenant cannot go as our mother — can he?"

They all laughed.

"No," replied Mr. Percy; "but a family

ticket means a company ticket, and if they were all men it would make no difference."

The ticket was secured, berths were taken, and the next evening about dark the steamer sailed. She was anchored in the harbor of Naples, and the party were carried out in boats, and in the operation almost swamped. So careless was the boatman, that Mr. Tenant lost his good nature, and reproved the fellow somewhat sharply.

That night, when they retired to rest, the moon and stars were shining brightly, and they anticipated a delightful run up the Mediterranean. But, about midnight, Walter woke by the violent pitching of the vessel, and found the cabin in much confusion. His father was already up, and very seasick. Minnie was in the ladies' cabin, in charge of Mrs. Seymour, and Mr. Tenant, who was never seasick, was in his berth laughing at the sorrowful figure presented by his friend.

" What is the matter, father ? " asked Walter.

No answer.

" Is it a storm ? "

No reply.

Just then a terrific peal of thunder that seemed to break about the steamer, gave him the information he desired. It was one of those dreadful thunder storms that sometimes range over the blue waters of the Mediterranean like an angry demon, raging with uncontrollable fury. There were about forty of them in the cabin, a little, square room, not large enough to accommodate twenty comfortably. The waves dashed over the decks, and the passengers were shut down, with little ventilation. The steamer was small, and, under the violence of the waves, seemed to be knocked about like a chip in a tempest. The little boat seemed to be standing now on one end, and then on the other; now poised on a watery pinnacle, and anon buried deep in the trough of the sea, while far above her the angry waves were heard roaring in their terrible might. Mr. Percy was too sick to be afraid, and Walter, leaving his own berth, crept into that of Mr. Tenant, who kept him from being thrown out violently.

But all at once a crash was heard on deck; terrific yells sounded from above, and it seemed as if the steamer was going down. In an instant every person was on his feet, and every berth left vacant.

"We are gone for it, Walter," said Mr. Tenant, holding the lad firmly.

"O, dear, dear, boo, boo, boo!" moaned a stout man, who was holding on to his berth.

"We are sinking; help! help!" shouted an Englishman, running to the stairway.

"*De quoi s'agit-il là?*" (what's the matter there?) cried a Frenchman, leaping from his berth.

For a few minutes the wildest consternation reigned in the cabin. No one seemed to know what the matter was; but most of the passengers thought they were going to the bottom. But that catastrophe not happening at once, some of the more active managed to open the gangway and get on deck, where the trouble was at once explained.

"What was it?" asked twenty persons at once, as they came down again, drenched with water, and wet to the skin.

"O, nothing at all," replied one.

"But tell us," cried the excited passengers.

"Right over our heads," said Mr. Tenant, who had been one of the three who had been on deck, "a dozen horses were fastened. During one of the lurches of the vessel the stalls in which they were confined gave way, and the affrighted animals went capering about the deck, to the consternation of their Italian keepers, who set up the fearful howl we heard."

"Is that all?" asked the stout man who had boo-hoo'd so loudly.

"I thought it was nothing," said the Englishman who had cried for help.

"*Très bien*," (very well,) muttered the Frenchman, jumping into his berth.

The wind now going down, and the storm subsiding, Mr. Tenant went to his berth, taking Walter with him, as Mr. Percy was very sick.

"What became of the horses?" asked Walter.

"They went overboard — all of them. But go to sleep, the steamer does not pitch much now."

Walter slept soundly, and woke in the morning to find the sun shining, and the sea as smooth as if it had never known a storm; and in due time the little steamer rode into the harbor of Leghorn, which is a dull place, the stores and houses all bearing marks of decay. Business seemed to be stagnant and dead, and they walked about amid deserted habitations and silent streets.

At Leghorn the steamer was to stop all day to take in freight, and our travellers improved it by a visit to Pisa, about twelve miles distant, and which is reached by rail. The first thing after arriving at Pisa was to visit the wonderful leaning tower, which has seven bells, and is two hundred and seventy-eight feet high.

"Do we go up, pa?" asked Minnie.

COASTWISE.

"Yes."

"How?"

"We ascend by a winding staircase, and from the top enjoy a fine prospect of the surrounding country."

And up they went, until Minnie's little ankles were tired, and Walter began to pant with the exertion, and at length they were at the top.

"How much does it lean over?" asked Walter of his father.

"The declination is from fifteen to eighteen feet."

"How came it to lean so?"

"Whether the tower was built as it is, in a leaning position, or whether the foundations have settled, is a matter of question, nor can an examination settle the point. I incline to the latter opinion, which accords with the view taken by most travellers."

"I want to go down?" said Minnie.

"What for?" asked Walter.

"O, I am dizzy."

"Folly!"

"No, it is not folly; I am real dizzy!"

"Then don't look over."

No wonder Minnie was dizzy. One naturally clings to the rail of the gallery as he looks down from the dizzy elevation upon the earth beneath, which seems to be passing from under him.

When they had staid up there long enough, they descended and went to the cathedral, the interior of which is of alternate layers of black and white marble, giving it a unique appearance. The dome is finely frescoed, and fine paintings adorn the walls.

"Look at that chandelier, children," said Mr. Percy.

"Yes, sir, I see," replied Walter.

"That is not much," said Minnie.

"It is much," said her father, reprovingly.

"What makes it?"

"I will tell you. That chandelier, once beautiful, but now black and time-worn, and suspended from the centre of the dome above by a black, dirty rope, suggested to Galileo the idea of the pendulum, which has since been applied to so much advantage to the world."

"Ah!" said Walter, quite pleased with the information.

"O, O!" cried Minnie.

"What is the matter, child?" asked Mr. Tenant.

"O, see that creature!"

"Don't be frightened."

"See that spear in his hand."

THE DORIA PALACE, GENOA.

"Ah, that is a monk, with his face covered with a black nightcap, with holes for his hateful eyes to glare out, come to beg; and what you thought was a spear, is a collection box."

"O, I thought it was—the—the—wicked one."

"Hush, child," said her father.

The monk did certainly look frightful, with his black mask covering his face.

The party went to the baptistery, a large and elegant building in the form of an immense dome, which rises to a height of one hundred and seventy-nine feet; and to the Campo Santo, in which they were all much interested, and then returned to Leghorn, where, at night, they again embarked for Genoa, at which place they arrived the next morning, all glad to leave the little miserable steamer.

"Why do you call this a city of palaces?" asked Walter of his father one night while in Genoa.

"Because palaces are so numerous here."

"We have seen several; but not enough to make the city remarkable on account of them."

"They are more numerous than you suppose. These hotels that you see were once the palaces of nobles and princes. Any person may rent a palace at a less cost than he can hire a decent tenement among us; and beggars now tread where nobles used to live."

"Columbus used to live here."

"Yes."

"Was he the son of a noble?"

"Yes, a noble wool-comber."

"Tell us about Columbus," said Minnie.

"He was born poor, and struggled with poverty all through his youth. In 1470 he went to Lisbon, married a wealthy lady, and devoted himself to geographical pursuits. When he became convinced that there was an undiscovered continent, he laid his plans before the Portuguese court, but they were rejected. He then came home to Genoa; but this city refused the honor. He then went to the court of Spain, and at length, after numerous discouragements, set sail from Palos, under the patronage of Ferdinand and Isabella."

"How old was he?"

"In his fifty-sixth year."

"You have both read about the discovery, how the sailors wanted to return, and for weeks murmured against him; how at length the birds from the land were seen, then a branch with red berries on it. When Columbus had taken possession of St. Salvador he returned to Spain, where a triumphant reception met him; and he marched beneath a bower bearing the inscription, —

> Por Castilla y por Leon
> Nuevo Mundo hallo Colon.'"

"What does that mean?"

"It means, 'For Castile and Leon Columbus has discovered a new world.'"

"Why did they not call our country, 'Columbia,' for him?"

"Because the honor was unjustly claimed by another adventurer."

"Who?"

"Amerigo Vespucci."

"How did Columbus die?"

"In disgrace, from the ingratitude of Spain."

"Tell us more about him."

"No, not to-night. Retire now, and rest."

"Good night, father," said Walter.

"Good night," said Minnie.

"Good night, and pleasant dreams to you both."

Chapter XVIII.

GLIMPSES OF BATTLE.

THE beautiful plains of Italy have often been drenched in blood. Some of the most terrible battles ever fought, have been witnessed on that devoted peninsula; and ere the people are free from tyrants, new streams of human gore will doubtless flow, and new scenes of carnage will be witnessed. Our party arrived in the north of Italy while those stirring events, which have already become parts of written history, were transpiring in 1859.

"I have a proposition to make," said Mr. Percy, one morning just after reaching Turin.

"What may it be, pa?" asked Minnie.

"It *may* be to put you into a convent," said Walter, laughing.

"I don't think I should consent to that. But what *is* it, father?"

"It is to leave you in Turin, while the rest of us go out to where the French army is encamped, and see what is going on."

"*Vive l'Empereur!*" shouted Walter, delighted with the proposition.

"What will you do with me?" asked Minnie.

"Leave you here."

"Alone?"

"No."

"Who with?"

"I saw yesterday a family from Boston, who are to remain in Turin several weeks, and they say they would be glad to take care of Minnie, and do for her more than her father can."

"Who are they?"

"A family named Phillips, consisting of husband and wife and two daughters."

"How old are the daughters?"

"One seventeen, and the other fifteen years."

"Are they pleasant people?"

"Yes."

"How long will you be gone?"

"But a few days. What do you think of it?"

"I can stay; but I would rather go with you."

"No; that would not do at all."

"Then I will stay here. When will you start?"

"To-morrow morning, if Mr. Tenant agrees to it."

"I certainly do," said that gentleman, who had been entertaining the same ideas.

So, the next morning Minnie was introduced to the family, with which she was to stay during the absence of the party; and the rest of the company started for the field of battle.

"Who is this Garibaldi that I hear so much about?" asked Walter of Mr. Tenant.

"He seems to be a very prominent character in this campaign."

"Well, tell me all about him, so when I read about him I shall know who he is."

"He was born at Nice, on the 4th of July, 1807."

"Famous day for a patriot to be born."

"Yes."

"Who was his father?"

"His family was poor; his father an unknown man; and he was brought up among the fishermen of his native place. He entered the Sardinian navy at an early age, and soon distinguished himself. But let me read a few passages from his life, written by one who knows him well."

"Read on."

"'Implicated in 1834 in the Italian insurrectional movement, this young seaman, compromised at Genoa on account of a Liberal conspiracy, found himself compelled to take refuge in France. He travelled on foot across the mountains to Nice, where he lay concealed two days in a friend's house, who, by dressing him in the clothes of a farmer of his, got him across the Var. After passing two years at Marseilles, chiefly in the pursuit of his mathematical studies, Garibaldi embarked in an Egyptian corvette, to go and serve as a naval officer in the fleet of the Bey of Tunis. As he did not meet there with a part to satisfy his active mind, he could not remain longer than a few months. So he soon set out for Rio Janeiro. The province of Rio Grande del Sol had erected itself into a republic. Our adventurer made an offer of his sword to the military government of Uruguay, and received the chief command of the squadron intended to act against Buenos Ayres. The contest lasted two years. During this time the new commander, quite in his element, performed such prodigies of valor that the natives said of him, 'It is not a man, but a devil;' and so superstition got mixed up with his name. He had been seen in several encounters to dash with his troops into the thick of the fight, then reappear safe and sound, and always victorious, from these terrible engagements, where the fighting was always hand to hand.'"

"But how came he back to Italy?"

"The account tells, 'The insurrection of the peninsula, in 1848, brought Garibaldi back to

Nice. A part of his legion accompanied him; with it he acted prominently in the war of independence against the Austrians in the Southern Tyrol, where, as a sharpshooter, he incessantly harassed their army. At Rome, he was the soul of the resistance. Marshal Vaillant, in his report of the operations during the siege, did justice to the energy and skill of his adversary. It was impossible, in fact, to make more of the poor resources left at the disposal of the besieged. The volunteers fought there like veteran troops. On the 9th of May, at Palestrina, he defeated the Neapolitan army, twice superior in numbers to his own. A few days later, at Velletri, where he was severely wounded, he was still to win the honors of the day. Finally, he sustained for a whole month the attacks of the French army, and, as all the officers admit, with admirable presence of mind. In the last council of war held at Rome, Garibaldi, on being called upon to give his opinion, proposed the employment of extreme measures; but they were not approved. He then left the city with the remnant of his little army, traversed the enemy's lines, and withdrew to the neighborhood of St. Marin. There his troops disbanded.'"

"Was he not in America a while?"

"Yes, he went to America and engaged in

trade for a time, and then went to Peru, where he again distinguished himself in the army. When the war was over he returned to Italy, and lived in quiet on the Island of Caprea."

" What about his family ? "

" He had a lovely wife, who was a heroine indeed. She went with him into battle, and was killed at his side."

" By whom ?."

" By the Austrians."

" They will kill him by and by — won't they ? "

" Very likely; but he seems now destined to play a very important part in the regeneration of Italy."

As they journeyed through the country, Walter obtained much information in relation to the movements of the hero and the allied armies. The party passed on until they began to see the evidences of war. They crossed the Ticino at Buffalora, and saw the wonderful bridge which was destroyed by the Sardinians, having been blown up by gunpowder. It was one thousand feet long, and cost seven hundred thousand dollars. It was called the Everlasting Bridge, as it was designed to last forever. On through Milan and Bergamo they went to Brescia; and here they paused to form plans and consider what had better be done. When they had reached a conclusion, they went on by a circuitous route to Castiglione, a town on the hill-side, where they found out the positions of the two armies. Then they cautiously followed through a country filled with dangers, and at a safe distance witnessed the great battle of Solferino. The village by this name is built around a conical hill, on the top of which is the Spia d' Italia, a square tower, from the top of which you can see the whole country, from the Po to the Alps. Following upon the rear of the French, putting themselves under military protection, but careful to keep far enough from actual peril, they saw the battle, as well as they could see, without being engaged in it. The furious charges, the terrible resistance, the final result, were all witnessed. The fight was for the village, and the Austrians were forced back by degrees, contending step by step. Walter was horror-struck to see the shells bursting in the midst of crowds of men, scattering death all around.

"How many soldiers are there engaged?" asked Walter of his father, as they stood looking through glasses at the battle.

"There must be as many as three hundred thousand."

"How does this number compare with other battles?"

"What ones?"

"Any of the battles of the first Napoleon — say Waterloo?"

"At Waterloo, as I told you on the field when we went on it, there were sixty-seven thousand French and sixty thousand English, and Blucher brought up the reserve of about thirty thousand Prussians."

"How many were there at Austerlitz?"

"About seventy thousand French, seventy thousand Austrians, and fourteen thousand Russians."

"At Wagram?"

"The French had one hundred and seventy thousand, and the Austrians one hundred and thirty-seven thousand."

"At Moscow?"

"The Russians had one hundred and thirty thousand men and six hundred pieces of cannon, the French one hundred and thirty-four thousand men and five hundred and eighty-seven cannon; the former lost fifty-eight thousand and the latter fifty thousand."

"At Leipsic?"

"At the battle of Leipsic, the three hundred and thirty thousand allies had against them two hundred and sixty thousand French; the latter lost thirty thousand prisoners and forty-five thousand killed and wounded, and the former forty-eight thousand killed and wounded."

" How was it at Jena ? "

" There there were one hundred and forty-two thousand French and one hundred and fifty-two thousand Prussians."

While they were gazing on, they saw the Austrians give way before the intrepid French, and soon they were advancing towards the town. All along were dead bodies, and the sickening sight led Walter to desire to be taken away from the scene of carnage and blood. Believing it safer to retire, not knowing what excesses would be committed after the battle, the party returned to Castiglione, where they passed the night. The next day they wandered over the battle-field, and went into the riddled village of Solferino. Every where they were treated with courtesy, and a French officer paid them every attention in his power.

When they had seen enough, they took a circuitous route, and returned to Turin, where they found Minnie lonesome and sad; but she was soon cheered by their presence. Walter gave her a long account of what he had seen.

" Did you see Victor Emmanuel ? "

" Yes, sis."

" How did he look ? "

"He is a robust man, with heavy whiskers, and a brave look, and — and — I don't know how he looked."

"Did you see the emperor?"

"What emperor?"

"Napoleon."

"Yes, several times."

"The Emperor of Austria — did you see him?"

"No, we did not dare to go where he was. We took good care to keep out of the way of the Austrians."

"Did you hear how he felt when he found that he was beaten."

"We were told in Milan that he wept like a child."

"What a baby!"

"Men of stronger minds than his have wept when the tide of battle has turned against them."

A few days after this, they heard that the two emperors had had an interview at Villafranca, and concluded an armistice. The particulars were derived from official bulletins, and from the papers of the day. At length Mr. Tenant received a letter from an Englishman whose acquaintance he had made, and from that the party gathered some interesting facts not previously made public.

"Ah, see here, children, what I received."

"What is it, Mr. Tenant?" they both asked.

"A letter from that English letter writer, whom we met at Castiglione."

"What does he say? Read it to us."

"Well, listen to what he says about events that occurred subsequently to our leaving the scene of battle: —

"'The Emperor of the French, accompanied by Marshal Vaillant, Generals Martimprey and Fleury, his military household, the Cent Gardes, and a squadron of Guides, started at seven from Valleggio on horseback. He arrived at Villafranca, which is about five miles distant, after a slow and somewhat protracted journey, stopping on the way several times, and frequently riding out from the regular road. The meeting of the two sovereigns was fixed for nine o'clock. At a quarter of an hour before, Napoleon arrived at the spot; and he came before the time in order that he might go on for a short distance to meet the Emperor of Austria. Francis Joseph soon made his appearance, and seeing that his late adversary had courteously come to receive him, urged forward his horse. When the two parties had come near, the escorts stopped short, and the emperors advanced into the centre of the unoccupied space. The escort of Louis Napoleon was composed of Marshal Vaillant, General Martimprey, General Fleury, the officers of the imperial household, and of his staff, and of a squadron of the Cent Gardes, and one of the Guides, all in their splendid full-dress uniforms. He rode the fine bay horse which he has used since the commencement of the campaign, and wore the undress uniform of a general of division, in which he looks well. The Emperor of Austria wore an undress cap, and blue uniform frock coat, and was followed by his staff, a squadron of his body-guard, composed of nobles, and a squadron of Hulans. It is said that he was much struck with the martial bearing of the French cavalry, and that in presence of the Cent Gardes and the Guides, the Austrian body-guard and the Hulans did not appear to advantage. On the two sovereigns meeting in the mid space they courteously saluted and shook hands. The Emperor of Austria appeared pleased with the cordial welcome and open manner of the Emperor Napoleon. The two emperors remained for a moment alone in the middle of the road, and exchanged a few words. They then reciprocally presented the officers of their staffs; and the moment after the several officers were intermingled, and Marshal Vaillant was seen in conversation with Baron de Hess. Napoleon III.

and the Emperor Francis Joseph then advanced side by side towards Villafranca, the Cent Gardes giving the precedence to the body-guard of Austria, who led the way, but the Guides passing before the Hulans. At Villafranca, the house of M. Carlo Morelli, situated in the principal street of the town, had been prepared to receive the two sovereigns. The Emperor of Austria had passed a night there before the battle of Solferino. It is a habitation comfortable, but simple, and not remarkable for any extraordinary attraction. The furniture and curtains of the conference room were green, and the walls painted in distemper. There were several seats of various kinds, but only two arm chairs. In the centre was an oblong table covered with a green cloth, and on it was placed a vase of freshly-gathered flowers, which quite perfumed the room. It was there that for upwards of an hour and a half the two emperors were seated, discussing the highest interests, and without any one being present. The King of Piedmont was not invited to the interview. Whilst the interview was going on, I was outside in the street, whence I could see the escorts, some remaining seated on their horses, while others had dismounted, but not the slightest sound was heard; every kind of conversation was suspended, and all seemed dominated voluntarily by the importance of the incident which was passing. As to what took place inside I cannot say any thing; all that I know is, that when the two sovereigns issued forth from the conference, they seemed both perfectly satisfied. The word to mount was then given, and in an instant all were in the saddle. The Emperor of Austria uttered a few words expressive of the admiration he felt for the French army, and did Marshal Vaillant and Generals Martimprey and Fleury the honor of shaking hands with them. The two sovereigns then took leave of each other with the greatest cordiality, and the next moment each splendid *cortége* was on the way back to the place from which it had started. The Emperor of the French entered Valleggio a little after eleven.' "

"That is very interesting," said Walter, as Mr. Tenant folded up his letter.

"Yes; but what has become of Napoleon's boast, that he would give freedom to Italy from the Alps to the Adriatic," asked Mr. Percy.

"O," replied Mr. Tenant, "these monarchs act from matters of expediency, and change their minds as often as there seems to be a change of circumstances."

"That is so," said Mr. Leonard, a young

American, who was present; "for Napoleon has just made a speech in reply to an address given him, in which he is reported to have explained his course in the following words: 'Arrived beneath the walls of Verona, the struggle was inevitably about to change its nature, as well in a military as in a political aspect. Obliged to attack the enemy in front, who was intrenched behind great fortresses, and protected on his flank by the neutrality of the surrounding territory, and about to begin a long and barren war, I found myself in face of Europe in arms, ready either to dispute our successes or to aggravate our reverses. Nevertheless, the difficulty of the enterprise would not have shaken my resolution, if the means had not been out of proportion to the results to be expected. It was necessary to crush boldly the obstacles opposed by neutral territories, and then to accept a conflict on the Rhine as well as on the Adige. It was necessary to fortify ourselves openly with the concurrence of revolution. It was necessary to go on shedding precious blood, and at last risk that which a sovereign should only stake for the independence of his country. If I have stopped, it was neither through weariness or exhaustion, nor through abandoning the noble cause which I desired to serve, but in the interests of France.

I felt great reluctance to put reins upon the ardor of our soldiers, to retrench from my programme the territory from the Mincio to the Adriatic, and to see vanish from honest hearts noble illusions and patriotic hopes. In order to serve the independence of Italy I made war against the mind of Europe, and as soon as the destinies of my country might be endangered I concluded peace.'"

"I wonder what Francis Joseph says to his people in explanation of his defeat," said Walter.

"He has also sent a manifesto to his people," answered Mr. Leonard.

"What does he say?"

"He admits that the fortunes of war have not been favorable to him and his cause, but assures them that the French, in spite of the greatest efforts, in spite of the superior forces which they had for a long period been preparing for the conflict, have been able, even by making the greatest sacrifices, to obtain only advantages, not a decisive victory; while the Austrian army, still animated by the same ardor, and full of the same courage, maintained a position, the possession of which left perhaps a possibility of recovering from the enemy all the advantages that he had gained."

"Why didn't he go on with the war then?"

"He has his explanation."

"What is it?"

"He pretends to be very humane, and wishes to spare the shedding of blood, and says, 'In spite of the ardent sympathy, worthy of acknowledgment, which the justice of our cause has inspired, for the most part, in the governments and peoples of Germany, our natural allies, most ancient allies, have obstinately refused to recognize the great importance of the grand question of the day. Consequently, Austria would have been obliged all alone to face the events which were being prepared for, and which every day might have rendered more grave. The honor of Austria coming intact out of this war, thanks to the heroic efforts of her valiant army, I have resolved, yielding to political considerations, to make a sacrifice for the reëstablishment of peace, and to accept the preliminaries which ought to lead to its conclusion; for I have acquired the conviction that I should obtain, in any event, conditions less unfavorable in coming to a direct understanding with the Emperor of the French, without the blending of any third party whatsoever, than in causing to participate in the negotiations the three great powers which have taken no part in the struggle. Unhappily, I have been unable to escape the separation from the rest of the empire of the greater part of Lombardy. On the other hand, it must be agreeable to my heart to see the blessings of peace assured afresh to my beloved people; and these blessings are doubly precious to me, because they will give me the necessary leisure for bestowing henceforth without distraction all my attention and solicitude on the fruitful task that I propose to accomplish; that is to say, to found in a durable manner the internal well-being and the external power of Austria by the happy development of her moral and material forces, and by ameliorations conformable to the spirit of the time in legislation and administration.'"

"Victor Emmanuel must feel badly in view of this?"

"No, he does not seem to."

"How do you know?"

"I saw posted in the streets to-day his proclamation, in which he seems jubilant at the conclusion of the war. He says he has come back from battle to tell the nation that Heaven has granted its wishes. He calls Napoleon 'a magnanimous and valiant ally.'"

"There is one other," said Walter, "who does not seem to have been consulted."

"Who is that?" asked Mr. Percy.

"Garibaldi."

"No; his name does not appear to have been mentioned in the matter."

"What will he do?"

"It is hard to tell. His idea of a free and united Italy is not yet realized, and he will probably fight on his own charges."

"Where will he be likely to make his appearance?"

"Perhaps in the vicinity of Venice; perhaps beneath the walls of Rome; perhaps in the streets of Naples."

"Can he do any thing alone?"

"He is not alone. Right is with him; God is with him; the sympathy of Italy is with him."

"What makes him hate the Austrians so badly?"

"He has been ill-treated by them, as you know, and he will not rest until Austrian influence is swept out of Italy."

"I heard an anecdote of him the other day."

"What was it, my son?"

"At one time since the commencement of hostilities, General Urban had one of Garibaldi's men shot. Garibaldi at the time had twenty-two Austrian prisoners, and when he heard what Urban had done, he gave orders to shoot two of them, and then calling the oldest of the prisoners before him, said, 'I set you at liberty. Return to General Urban, and tell him that since he has caused one of my soldiers to be shot, I have shot two of his; and let him be assured that if I learn that a single prisoner is executed again, I swear to shoot every one who may fall into my hands, be he marshal or Emperor of Austria. Let him not force me to show what the wrath of a father, whose child, scarcely aged thirteen, was assassinated by Austrian soldiers, may drive him to do.'"

"Would he dare do that?" asked Minnie.

"He would *dare* do any thing, I should think," replied her brother.

"But if he should shoot the emperor, all Europe would rise up against him."

"So father says."

"But, perhaps, while kings and courts rose up against him," said Mr. Leonard, "all the people might rise up for him. It would take but a spark to set this whole continent in a blaze."

"O, I shudder at the idea," said Minnie. "It seems so dreadful."

"Yet not so dreadful as the continued oppression of this whole land. Italy is under a curse, and blood will be shed to wipe it off; and it is not so fearful to have the blood flow as to have these millions forever trampled under foot. All good men would rejoice in the emancipation of this peninsula."

"Did you not say, father, that Garibaldi was in America once?"

"Yes."

"Was he in Boston?"

"Yes; he came to Boston in the year 1853 as the captain of a Peruvian bark."

"What was her name?"

"The Carmen."

"I should like to see him."

"It is doubtful if you ever will."

"Why not?"

"Because we are so soon to leave this land, and he will probably live here until, in some convulsion of the political elements, he will lose his life."

"O, I hope not!"

"So do I."

"And so does half the world," added Mr. Tenant. "On the life of this brave man hang the most important events — perhaps the future destinies of Italy."

"Is not this people changed very much?" asked Minnie, "since the old times of which I have read?"

"O, yes. As the traveller pursues his way from the palaces of Naples up to the foot of the

Alps, he forgets, in the present degradation of the people, that this is the land of Dante, Michael Angelo, Petrarch, and Manzoni."

"What has done it?"

"You who have looked upon Italy as it is, without knowing much of its history, and its political condition, fail, of course, to see why it is, and I have hardly time to go into the subject. But you see it as it is — a besotted region. The finest of all lands, it lies under a bitter curse. The hand of God is on it, withering its flowers and threatening woe to the people. Priestcraft and kingcraft are doing what foreign armies and invading forces never could do. The despot's foot is on the track of progress, and his iron hand is raised against the spread of truth."

"Do you suppose it will ever be free?"

"Yes, all lands will eventually be free."

And the young reader who has heard of Garibaldi, and the struggles for Italian independence, ever must wish that Italy may become independent, and that the words of Mr. Percy may prove true. Even children love liberty, and those boys and girls who know how much the old soldiers of the revolution suffered for liberty, must wish that so beautiful a country as Italy might have the same freedom that is enjoyed in New England. And perhaps she will soon.

"Voices from the mountains speak;
 Apennines to Alps reply;
 Vale to vale, and peak to peak,
 Toss an old remembered cry:
  Italy
  Shall be free;
 Such the mighty shout that fills
 All the passes of her hills."

We have now followed our travellers through several most interesting countries, and with them witnessed many very interesting things; and now, while the last page of this little volume is being written, the very changes spoken of by Mr. Percy to his children are taking place. The young reader will not need to be informed that Garibaldi has, with a few undisciplined regiments, driven the Neapolitan army from Sicily, and, marching on Naples, the king fled to Gaeta, (to which town the reader will remember the children were told the pope fled, in 1848, in disgrace,) and the conqueror entered with a loss of only eight men, leaving his army at a distance, while he rode with his suite through the streets crowded with men who had so lately been hostile to him.

And still, ere the page is closed, the wonderful intelligence comes that Rome, that stagnant sea, is stirred, that the pope meditates flight, that the papal troops are flying before the Sardinians, and that the Eternal City is rocking like the cradle of revolution.

>"Long ago was Gracchus slain;
>   Brutus perished long ago;
> Yet the living roots remain
>   Whence the shoots of greatness grow.
>   Yet again,
>   Godlike men,
> Sprung from that heroic stem,
> Call the land to rise with them.
>
>"They who haunt the swarming street,
>   They who chase the mountain boar,
> Or, where cliff and billow meet,
>   Prune the vine or pull the oar,
>   With a stroke
>   Break their yoke;
> Slaves but yester-eve were they —
> Freemen with the dawning day.
>
>"Looking in his children's eyes,
>   While his own with gladness flash,
> 'Ne'er shall these,' the father cries,
>   'Cringe, like hounds, beneath the lash.
>   These shall ne'er
>   Brook to wear
> Chains that, thick with sordid rust,
> Weigh the spirit to the dust.'
>
>"Monarchs, ye whose armies stand
>   Harnessed for the battle field,
> Pause, and from the lifted hand
>   Drop the bolts of war ye wield.
>   Stand aloof
>   While the proof

Of the people's might is given;
Leave their kings to them and heaven.

"Stand aloof, and see the oppressed
　Chase the oppressor, pale with fear,
As the fresh winds of the west
　Blow the misty valleys clear.
　　Stand and see
　　Italy
Cast the gyves she wears no more
To the gulfs that steep her shore."

So writes a poet of our own land; and to every noble sentiment the childhood, as well as the manhood, of America will joyfully respond. The words that Walter wrote in his journal, the last night of his stay in Turin, before leaving for Milan, will be echoed by all our youthful readers: "May revolution go on until the mailed heel of Victor Emmanuel shall clank upon the marble pavement of the Vatican, and Garibaldi shall cross the Rialto, and be welcomed as the deliverer of Venetia, and Kossuth shall wave the banner of Arpad over regenerated Hungary, and all the world shall be free."

www.ingramcontent.com/pod-product-compliance
Lightning Source LLC
Chambersburg PA
CBHW020758230426
43666CB00007B/750